RITUALIZATION AND HUMAN INTERIORITY

RITUALIZATION
AND HUMAN
INTERIORITY

Clemens Cavallin

Museum Tusculanum Press
University of Copenhagen
2013

Ritualization and Human Interiority

© Museum Tusculanum Press and Clemens Cavallin, 2013

Consultant: Mikael Aktor

Composition and cover design: Erling Lynder

Set in Quadraat

ISBN 978 87 635 3734 6

This volume is published with financial support from
The Swedish Research Council

Museum Tusculanum Press

Birketinget 6

DK-2300 Copenhagen S

Denmark

www.mtp.dk

Contents

Acknowledgments

I began to write on the topic of ritual interiorization at the same time as I temporarily left Sweden in 2003 to work for three and a half years at the University of Bergen, which is situated on the beautiful west coast of Norway. There the section of History of Religions, within the larger structure of the now defunct IKRR, provided a stimulating milieu where the first draft of this book was written. I especially want to express my gratitude to Professor Håkan Rydving who read the manuscript in its entirety and gave me vital encouragement and many helpful suggestions on how to improve the text. Memorable in Bergen was also the discussions at Parkveien over a bowl of soup or a Caesar salad with Dom Elias Carr, who has continued to act as an intellectual dialogue partner after my relocation to Sweden in 2007, and his return to Austria and subsequent move to New York.

While in Norway, I also briefly benefited from the exciting milieu in Oslo cultivated by Professor Jens Braarvig in connection with his work on the Schøyen Collection.

To my father I owe a debt of gratitude, particularly due to our conversations on intentionality in a legal context, which is still an ongoing discourse evolving with the unfolding of life, but this acknowledgment is also motivated by many other acts of assistance on the part of him and my mother that have made this work possible.

Finally, I dedicate this book to my wife Natalie and our children, who have never wavered in their trust that this work would bear fruit in due time.

Abstract

Bringing the topics of human interiority and ritual together can at first glance appear as a strategy for establishing a basic theme of antagonism between the inner and the outer aspects of human actions. The main thesis of this study is, however, that although the depiction of interiorization and ritualization as opposing powers contains some elements of truth, the most vital aspects of their relationship are to be found in their dynamic interdependence.

The basic account of ritualization takes as its point of departure the notion of abstract action in the ritual theory of Caroline Humphrey and James Laidlaw. The abstract quality of an action refers to the performance of a ritual as disconnected from its context, that the action is more directed toward its own performance than outside goals. This aspect of ritual action can also be connected with conceptual abstraction. According to the perspective on ritual action elaborated in this study, the particular efficacy of ritualized acts, persons, and artifacts is an effect of the fact that the abstraction achieved by ritualization provides a place for the performer in the world of ideal, abstract entities, allowing for a person to enter into relations with them.

The potential for deritualization by interiorization, however, reaches its peak when the ritual act is performed in the interior, its goal is interior, and its efficacy is completely derived from interior principles. In this way, the ritual has no real relevance outside of the individual, the very opposite of hyper-ritualization. But the final link still attaching this interior ritual to intersubjective ritual norms is severed by individualism, when the individual takes it upon itself to decide when or how to perform the ritual—in which case the ritual commitment vanishes and deritualization moves toward its completion. And, in all this, it is difficult not to perceive a profile of modernity emerging which presses toward the interior in search of the really real and a secure foundation for knowledge, but becomes frustrated by the elusive nature of the hidden and subjective.

Introduction

Bringing the topics of human interiority and ritual together within the covers of a scholarly study could at first glance appear as a strategy for establishing a basic theme of antagonism—in the sense of illustrating how ritualization drives religious behavior toward what is external and impersonal while its opposite force, interiorization, tends toward the realm of the subjective. In the Western cultural sphere, this division is often connected to a powerful discourse of authenticity which emphasizes the interiority of individuals as the authentic starting point for action, for example their conscience, while rituals are merely sterile repetitive actions that alienate individuals from both the deliberations of their autonomous reason and the depths of their emotional life (cf. Taylor 1991). The main thesis of this study is that although the depiction of interiorization and ritualization as opposing powers contains some elements of truth, the most vital aspects of their relationship are to be found in their interdependence—that, in fact, religious traditions inevitably have to live out this dynamism between interiority and ritual performance, even though some of them try to achieve either a completely interior worship untainted by formalized actions, or on the contrary strive to uphold a system of ritual activity that is believed to work independently of the emotional and cognitive life of the individual performer.

The emergence and consolidation of ritual studies as an interdisciplinary field of study during the late twentieth century quite naturally influenced religious studies (cf. Grimes 1995 [1982], xi; Bell 1997), and as a consequence helped to reinforce an increasingly stronger focus on concrete behavior in opposition to beliefs and theology, and in the long run also mythology—the analytic searchlight moving in this way from orthodoxy to orthopraxy (Watson 2007). Through their concrete nature, rituals seemed to some to offer a sounder way for scholarship to proceed in opposition to more or less speculative symbolical analyses.[1] Fritz Staal's idea of a radical split between ritual behavior and meaning ("the meaninglessness of ritual") was, therefore, though contested, symptomatic of a more general trend (Staal 1989; Rappaport 1997, 29–31; Stausberg 2002, 21–22; Michaels 2006).

The prominent place now given to rituals in the scholarly consideration of religion can also be seen as a corrective to the rather one-sided attention devoted to myths and symbolism in the hermeneutical approach of Mircea Eliade, the most prominent representative of the phenomenology of religion in the second half of the twentieth century (cf. Allen 1998). This ritual turn coincided with a growing criticism of the phenomenological magnanimous gesture of giving the believer's perspective pride of place; instead the contrary strategy grew in importance, aimed at situating religious discourse and praxis in a web of more or less unconscious constraining features of a sociological, psychological, or biological nature. The combined force of these two departures from the phenomenological paradigm led to semantic content of religious narrative being demoted from the center of theoretical interest. In an article on the myth and ritual theory, Robert Segal, therefore, when sketching a future for the theory, chooses to quote Gregory Nagy in an attempt to argue that myths are foremost instances of performance, and consequently forms of ritual (Segal 2006, 121). Such a ritualization of myth is the opposite strategy of envisioning rituals as texts, something which, on the other hand, can deprive rituals of their performative character, as they are treated as documents to be decoded, and not as efficacious actions.

However, when myths are seen as actions, as being intrinsically of a ritual nature, the tension between textuality and ritual performance is not overcome (cf. Bell 1992). The dilemma arises inevitably, though often remaining implicit, as ritualization of an action introduces a cleavage between meaning and correct performance, a point persuasively argued

---

[1]   At the same time, as remarked by Jens Kreinath (2005), when the semantic dimension is considered as merely attached, more or less arbitrarily, to ritual action, ritual studies is constituted as a separate field of research with its own object, ritual as such. To criticize the foundational separation of semantics from ritual grammar is hence tantamount to undermining the whole project of ritual studies.

by Caroline Humphrey and James Laidlaw in their theory of ritual action (Humphrey and Laidlaw 1994; 2006, 274). To aim at understanding rituals *qua* rituals then entails a concern with the syntax of religious action to the expense of semantic aspects as symbolism and narrativity. In this way, religious beliefs, and especially those espoused by a text-based elite cadre of theologians, are considered as only arbitrarily connected to ritual practice, and of little explanatory value.

When approaching cases of ritual interiorization, that is, instances of focusing on the interior of the human person within a ritual setting, one cannot, however, limit the scholarly attention to the structure of ritual actions, or to unconscious constraints, or how ritual actions are embedded within social structures. These perspectives have to be integrated with attempts at understanding and analyzing religious discourse. Otherwise this particular aspect of ritualized action will be out of analytical focus, as the management of human interiority within the frame of ritual proceedings takes the form of embodied and discursive practices turning the ritual toward the inner life of the individual. Such processes can seem to logically counteract ritualization, which de-emphasizes individuals and their subjective sphere, a feature that can be taken as indicating a close connection between interiorization and deritualization. However, when one looks more closely at what ritual interiorization can mean (conceptual clarification) and at examples covered by the notion (empirical investigation), a more nuanced and varied set of possible relations emerges. In this way, a picture is delineated that reflects the tensions between subjective and intersubjective; bodily exterior and interior; mind and world. An engagement with interiorizing tendencies in ritual traditions, therefore, functions as a counterweight to the theoretical attention directed toward exteriorizing aspects of ritual practice which makes human interiority and individuality marginal.

In order to argue for the interconnected nature of interiorization and ritualization, it is necessary to offer a theoretical account of ritual activity that has this dynamic relationship between interiority and exteriority at heart. The starting point in chapter one is, therefore, Caroline Humphrey and James Laidlaw's theory of ritualization that defines this process as a special modification of action, which ironically is a conscious renunciation of individual intention, thereby making the ritualized act independent of the intentionality of the ritual performer for its identity.[2] I present my own position on ritualization as a development of the notion of abstract action that Humphrey and Laidlaw in their turn borrowed from the French philosopher Merleau-Ponty. In this way, conceptual abstraction is linked to the formality of the ritual acts, opening up for a connection between the accounts of ritual as symbolic action and the portrayal of ritual as correct performance.

The account of ritualization in chapter one is followed by a similar characterization of interiorization in chapter two. Much of the bulk of that chapter is taken up by the presentation of different forms of interiorization, as various aspects of ritual actions can be interiorized, for example their efficacy or effects. This makes it possible in chapter three to work out a more nuanced and fine-grained sketch of the various forms of interaction between ritualization and interiorization than would otherwise have been possible. Though the overall intention of this book is to provide a theoretical model of precisely this dynamic relationship between interiority and exteriority within ritual traditions, also the question of the connection between deritualization and interiorization has to be addressed. And an almost inevitable extension of that theme is the subject of modernity and interiority, which constitutes the focus of the last chapter. It is important to note that the typically modern versions of interiorization are merely variants on a universal theme present in varying degrees in all ritual traditions. There were thus deritualizing potentialities also in premodern societies, but in the modern era this has taken on a quite particular and strong character. The discussion in the last chapter extends the discussion of interiorization by placing it in a wider context of modern self-reflexivity. Accordingly, with an implacable logic, the will to understand ritual traditions turns the analytical gaze toward the position

---

2   Cf. Gavin Flood's characterization of the ascetic renunciation of the self as an ironic act, which paradoxically produces a heightened form of subjectivity (e.g. Flood 2004, 14).

of the scholar himself and the larger venture of religious and ritual studies that he or she is part of.

SOME METHODOLOGICAL REMARKS

However, before embarking on the discussion of ritualization and interiorization, a few methodological remarks are in order as otherwise there can arise some ambiguity about where exactly the processes of interiorization are located. As this work is foremost conceptual in character and does not involve an intense in-depth analysis of a concrete ritual tradition, that topic tends not to emerge in the same way in the subsequent chapters as it would have done if the study had been foremost empirical in character. The remarks offered here are, therefore, primarily intended as an admonitory note to those setting out to investigate interiorization within a specific ritual tradition. It is necessary to differentiate between levels on which interiorization can occur, a task which is connected to the various types of sources available to us in the study of ritual traditions and innovations. This insight is vital for a valid analysis of interiorization, as an account in a text of a case of interiorization is not on the same level as that which we can observe in a concrete ritual performance, either first hand or on a video recording. Interiorization could, for example, in a contemporary religious text be a conscious rhetorical strategy used for the reinterpretation of ancient rituals which were originally very much focused on exterior aspects: in that way, the hermeneutist elaborates on the profound inner meaning of the ritual actions to the point where these become merely symbols for inner processes such as enlightenment or the cultivation of virtues. It seems, therefore, justified to single out in a first step two levels: that of ritual discourse and that of ritual practice,[3] which together constitute a larger whole, a ritual tradition. It is important that this is not understood as a demarcation between action and language in general, such as that between the act of igniting a fire and reciting a hymn to the god of fire. It is instead an attempt to distin-

3   The notion of practice is, in this context, not used as in the sociological theorizing of Bourdieu (cf. Bell 1992), but takes its primary inspiration from Margaret Archer's discussion of practical knowledge in relation to embodied and discursive knowledge (Archer 2000: 121–90).

guish between discourse about ritual and ritual action itself, the latter integrating both physical action and the use of more or less discursive language. The discourses intended to be singled out by the ritual practice/discourse distinction are thus those which take place outside the ritual frame and which are commentaries, in a loose sense, on those acts.

The distinction between ritual discourse and practice could be complicated by the fact that discussions on rituals become ritualized themselves, so that, for example, the discourse on one ritual is carried out in another ritual (cf. Stausberg 2006). Nevertheless, it is important that we uphold this distinction, because if we do not, we could start to draw conclusions and displace them too hastily from discourse on ritual to ritual action or from concrete rituals to discourse. Even if we often use ancient normative texts as clues to how sacrificial cults were performed, they do not necessarily reflect, in all respects, the actual ritual practice. For example, the paradigmatic example of ritual interiorization in the Christian world is the view, expressed both in the Old and New Testament, that it is not the outer aspects of rituals, such as the washing of hands, reading of prayers, or the sacrifice of an animal that are the prerequisites for the efficacy of the ritual acts, but it is a special mental (moral) attitude that is vital.[4] In that context, the interiorization of certain rituals is constituted by the prescribed connection between a mental attitude and the ritual gestures and formulas. However, it is not certain that the prescribed connection between mental attitude and gestures gains any widespread appeal, or is upheld with any constancy—as the moral quality of the intention is not easily decided upon since it is precisely interior, that is, not open to direct inspection.

Another problem with using normative liturgical texts as guides to practice is that it can be hard to distinguish between which norms were active and which were obsolete at a certain time period, as it cannot be assumed that revisions were necessarily carried out regularly and the obsolete norms vanished. If we find norms prescribing some form of interiorization, the question as to whether these norms at the time

---

4   See Ps. 50, Rom. 12.1–2, Heb. 13.16, 1 Pet. 2.5.

were rendered obsolete or not needs to be addressed. This is a different question than the one touching on the doubt as to what degree a norm prescribing a form of interiorization was in reality followed—since an obsolete norm is only normative in form, and considered by the community handling the text as outdated, or overruled by later norms.

To distinguish between discourse on ritual and actual ritual practice highlights not only the processes internal to the ritual tradition, but also alerts us to the methodological problem of arguing from sources on one level to conclusions on another. The dynamics of ritual discourse and practice is thus mirrored by the methodological difficulties of the scholar. If there is a high correspondence between discourse and ritual practice in a tradition, then textually fixed norms will be good indicators for the scholar of what in reality constituted the practice. If, however, there is a discrepancy between, for example, ritual manuals and practice, such a conclusion will not be valid. It is therefore important that we avoid conflating the levels on which interiorization occurs, and that we remain conscious about drawing conclusions from material on one level about proceedings and conferring them to a different level.

However, not all discourses on ritual are of the simple normative type establishing rules for ritual actions, but these prescriptions are often accompanied or embedded in ritual theology.[5] That is, an interiorizing interpretation does not specify directly how the ritual should be performed, "do this or that," but elaborates on the theme that these acts have a profound inner meaning. Such an interiorized meaning is not necessarily present in ritual practice, but the interpretation on the discourse level could be used *inter alia* as a strategy for making ancient sacrifices

---

5 Ritual theology (alternative liturgical theology) is here used in want of a better notion. Cf. Grimes (1995: 5) for a distinction between ritual study, liturgiology, and liturgics. It will in the following be used interchangeably with ritual ideology, although the latter does not in the same way indicate a discursive commentary on, or argumentation about, ritual. Theology should, moreover, not be understood here literally, i.e. as necessarily involving gods. Also the discussion of religious rituals as all powerful in themselves, or in relation to the backdrop of an impersonal principle or force field, would qualify as ritual theology in this wider sense. Another word which could be used is "ritualistics," but it, with its mythological connotation, signifies ambiguously both a religious collection of smaller discourses and a scholarly systematic approach to such discourses.

congenial to a modern mind, or as a way of opening up for an identification of contemporary rituals with older ones, and by this means explain-
ing the discontinuance of the older and perhaps more prestigious rituals.
Such a process is, for example, part of the legitimization of renunciation
in late Vedic and post Vedic Hindu theology, and "the very act and subsequent life of renunciation—which includes renunciation of sacrifice, of
ritual action, or *karman*—is presented in the texts as a 'higher' or 'truer'
sacrifice" (Smith 1998, 209).

The interpretation of a ritual can also be firmly grounded in actual
ritual practice or initiate a new more interiorized practice. In such a case,
the interpretation becomes normative in regulating the practice, indicating that at a deeper level interpretations of rituals are always normative
to some degree, and that perhaps a better distinction (than that between
normative and interpretive) is that between ritual manuals and ritual theology. However, the concept "ritual manual" denotes foremost a genre
of texts containing norms for regulating ritual practice, and although
providing a clear example of ritual normativity, it does not exhaust that
category.

Furthermore, if we turn to the level of practice and the question of interiorization on that level, we quickly run into problems of a methodological nature. For how are we to observe forms of interiorization in actual
ritual practice without inferring them from the content of ritual discourse? If we study ancient ritual traditions and have acquired an interesting piece of detailed ritual description, then we will see that interiorization processes to a high degree will be inferred from interpretations of
the ritual acts, as "now the priest is meditating on the goodness of God,"
while he perhaps instead is only counting to ten before continuing with
his manifest exterior actions. We are essentially in the same situation
when doing fieldwork: when a ritual tends to focus on what is inside the
ritual participants, in their inner bodies, or minds, the step to ritual ideology or ritual norms is inevitable as the scholar cannot perceive these
parts of the ritual, but must conclude from texts and oral comments that
this is what probably takes place. Interiorization is hence mediated to us
primarily through ritual discourse, as it is constituted by ritual processes

partially absorbed by the black hole of individuality—the subjective level of the intersubjectively organized ritual acts. We see this, for example, in the ritual of the Eucharist when the ritual participants swallow the bread or host, which thereby leaves the intersubjective physical body and enters into the inner body. To be able to witness a ritual is, therefore, not a guarantee allowing us to account for the processes of interiorization active in the ritual proceedings, as interiorization is a process toward what is interior, with other words, hidden and obscure. This does not only complicate matters for the scholar, but also for the ritual participants themselves. One example is the problem of knowing when a mentally performed ritual sequence is actually finished, or whether the "correct" mental attitude was present.

As a result, despite the attempt above to analytically differentiate the discourse level, or domain, from that of practice, forms of interiorization through their inner nature make practice methodologically secondary, which is not the same as ontologically secondary. That is, the inner is not more unreal by being more diffucult to observe, but it has to be inferred primarily by the externalization of interiority in exterior discourse.

CHAPTER ONE

Ritualization

As the word indicates, "ritualization" refers to the actual creation of ritual acts, or to the bestowal of a ritual character on otherwise non-ritual
acts. In her influential book *Ritual Theory, Ritual Practice,* Catherine Bell
gives a short review of the scholarly uses of the concept before presenting
her own approach which describes ritualization as a strategy for establishing privileged differentiations between different types of actions
within a culture (1992: 88–93). Thereby, neither formality nor repetition
are made into essential features of the rituals so constituted, instead
almost any strategy can be used that singles out an action as more prestigious or important than another. To this prestige, relations of power
are joined, making ritualization into a strategy for constructing and
subverting social structures. In order to avoid reified essences—and
like Thomas Tweed in his theory of religion (*Crossing and Dwelling,* 2006),
she chooses action nouns instead of nouns that refer to concrete and
abstract objects, in this way emphasizing the pragmatic, flowing character of ritual life. Her approach is helpful as it directs the attention of
the scholar toward the actual construction of ritual acts, but at the same
time it lacks in definitional strictness. Because when no essential feature
is given to qualify the action that has been set apart by the process of ritualization as precisely a ritual, then any strategy for differentiating some
actions—for example paying out extremely large amounts of money as
remuneration for services done to a company—could be viewed as a form
of ritualization. In the chapter "Characteristics of Ritual-like Activities"
in her later book *Ritual: Perspectives and Dimensions* (1997), she therefore
presents ways of ritualizing under headings such as "Formalism," "Tra-
ditionalism," and "Invariance." Nevertheless, she insists that "there is
no intrinsic or universal understandings of what constitutes ritual" (Bell
1997: 164). We are, hence, left with important insights into the nature of

ritualization, but also with a conceptual vagueness which makes it necessary to proceed and see if there is any possibility of retaining the action focus of ritualization, while at the same time increasing the definitional and theoretical rigor.

One promising avenue has been opened up by Caroline Humphrey and James Laidlaw in their study of the Jain pūjā (ritual offerings) from 1994. Already on the first page of the introduction they write that "[s]uch reactions therefore reveal the essential features of ritual action" (Humphrey and Laidlaw 1994: 1). However, although they do not shy away from essences in the same way as Bell, their analysis of the concept of ritual is similar in that they maintain that it "does not pick out a class of events or institutions in an analytically useful way" (1994: 3). The solution is, as it was for Bell, to opt for a theory of ritualization, focusing on the special transformation of action that this process entails. According to them, and as opposed to Bell, not any kind of differentiation of an action can be called an instance of ritualization. If for Bell the focus was on the privileged differentiation of actions and its connection to power, the basic problem laid out in their study is the relationship between ritual action and meaning.[6]

Humphrey and Laidlaw originally went to India in order to do research on the symbolism of the Jain pūjā, and they became intrigued by their informants' insistence that the rituals in themselves were empty, meaningless, while the meanings—which were abundant and diverse—had to be derived from the soul, that is, from the human interior. Humphrey and Laidlaw in this way met in the field a strategy of interiorization, where the meaning of the rituals were deemed interior by the performers rather than inherent in the actions and then simply decoded. This supplied the two scholars with an incitement to formulate a theory of ritual which has at its heart the notion that ritualization introduces a disjunction between the intentionality of the individual performer (i.e. his motive and purpose) and the intersubjective intention, the social definition of

---

6   They also distance themselves from Bell's use of the concept "practice," preferring instead "action" (1994: 4).

the type of action. The acts become in this way stipulated and acquire an "objective" existence (cf. Berger and Luckmann 1967); they are designed to be performed without being dependent upon the idiosyncrasies of the individual.

Normal actions are, on the other hand, characterized by intentionality; their nature is dependent upon the mental life of the agent, without which they would not be actions at all, merely movements or events. When an action is ritualized, intentionality is, however, not abolished, but transformed, as the performer through a ritual commitment comes to see the action as independent of his or her intentions and thoughts, as not relying upon them for its identity. The act comes preformed to the individual from the social context and insists upon the commitment of the individual.

The increase in distance between individual intentionality and social intention accomplished in ritualization lessens the impact of instrumental rationality in favor of normative rationality, which, however, does not mean that rituals lack in instrumental effectiveness (Humphrey and Laidlaw 1994: 12). When an action becomes ritualized, individual reason is not primarily engaged in a means-to-end calculation, but is subordinated to socially stipulated norms which tie down individual intention, to wit, the alternatives of acting. This is of course not an absolute condition, and rituals can in themselves be seen as means to an end, either by a social group, or by individuals, but it applies then to the ritual as a totality. If instrumental rationality would be consistently applied on an individual basis to a set of ritualized actions, then the characteristics of rituality would break down—the acts would become informal and idiosyncratic, losing their reified intersubjective status.[7]

---

7   A religious market situation is, however, not automatically unfavorable for ritualization, but instead enables the religious consumer to choose from a large supply of sets of ritualized actions. For the application of Rational Choice theory to religion, see Stark and Bainbridge 1996 [1987]. For an edited volume containing essays with a critical realist angle directing critique toward the Rational Choice paradigm, especially as it pertains to the relation between instrumental and value rationality, see Archer and Tritter 2000.

Since intentionality, however, is a somewhat too broad concept to give their theory precision, they differentiate between the intentional meaning of an action (i.e. its identity) and the prior purposes and motives for performing it. This is expressed as the distinction between intention *in* doing and intention *to* do an action (Humphrey and Laidlaw 1994: 93). The ritual stance severs the link connecting the motive, purpose, and general mental buzz of the ritual performer with the intentional meaning (intention in doing) and thus the identity of the act, which is constituted by the ritual commitment. That is, regardless of what the individual thinks while performing a ritual, for example the Jain pūjā, it is nevertheless still that very ritual. On the other hand, the categorization of an action as murder or manslaughter is dependent upon the motive of the individual.

ABSTRACT ACTION

An interesting concept discussed by Humphrey and Laidlaw is abstract action, a notion borrowed from Merleau-Ponty. The abstract quality of an action refers to the ritual being performed disconnected from its context, that the action is more directed toward its own performance than outside goals (Humphrey and Laidlaw 1994: 236–37). A special world of reified actions is in this way created. The doing away with the ordinary context of an action, thus making it abstract, is something which also Paul Ricoeur has discussed, but under the theme of analyzing actions as texts. He pinpoints the severance of individual intention and text (action) as the basic feature of the objectification of discourse. When moving from discourse to text, a process of fixation occurs which entails that "the author's intention and the meaning of the text cease to coincide" (Ricoeur 1973: 95; cf. Bell 1992: 51). The actual meaning of fixed discourse is then the worlds that it opens up, an almost unlimited spectrum of references. This is due to the fact that the original context of discourse is lacking—as simple ostentation is not possible as in the unfixed live oral discourse; furthermore, in a text, the dialogical partner is exchanged for a potentially unlimited audience. In extending this analysis of texts as fixed discourses to social action, a similar focus on action as disembedded occurs, the objectification of action. Humphrey and Laidlaw take up the same thread in regard to ritual action, turning our attention toward its severance from individuality, and creation as a social object.

While it is helpful to treat actions as texts, as Ricoeur does, I would like to take this analogy along a somewhat different road. The text metaphor primarily highlights the withdrawal of action from individual intention, but this abstract quality of ritual action can also be connected with conceptual abstraction, that is, the movement from the specific to the general, for example from the idea of the individual you, the reader, and, me, the writer, to the notion of a human being. In this process, most of the individual characteristics of you and me are taken away, and what remains is the idea of a "human being" that possesses some general qualities. The same process of abstraction takes place in the formulation of norms, for example those governing the Vedic sacrifices.[8] A norm is intended, in order to be a norm and not simply a command, to cover a more or less wide spectrum of behavior that takes place in different locations and at different times. The rules governing the Vedic Soma sacrifice, for example, have in common with the abstract notion of a "human being" that they are general, that is, abstracted from the irrelevant features of specific contexts. When a human being tries to conform to a general rule this demands some creative work of application, similar to the interpretation of a text, but what characterizes ritual action is that it tries to be like a norm, that it strives to eliminate the individual idiosyncrasies of the ritual participants: one could, in a ritual context, be expected to walk like an illustration of the abstract concept of walking, a kind of walking which is more at home in a platonic world of ideas than in everyday reality. This abstract quality of ritual actions is often referred to as formality, which Bell characterizes as "the use of a more limited and rigidly organized set of expressions and gestures, a 'restricted code' of communication and behaviour" (Bell 1997: 139).

There is a close connection between stylized theatrical *dramatis perso-*

---

8   The textual genre trying to formulate these norms in a systematic fashion is of course the Śrauta sūtras.

nae and the ritual person; they share this tendency of abstraction, of moving away from a particular context, a definite position in time and space, and striving toward an intersubjective world of abstract notions, social roles, and norms: all of which, however, to a high degree are instantiated in a narrative form and guided by the principle of personification. The individual in submitting to ritual norms acts out abstract actions which are part of an intersubjective repertoire of ideal notions and narratives. Ritual practice is not merely pure action to which meanings are arbitrarily connected, but action raised to the level of meaning itself. This is, as indicated above, a matter of degree—an action can become increasingly abstract, that is, ritualized, in the sense of being governed by norms. However, this formation of action is, as argued by Humphrey and Laidlaw, not always and probably more seldom accomplished by explicit discursive instruction and instead mostly effectuated through habituation with the help of mimesis, developing an embodied ritual know-how through imitating; learning by doing.

While Humphrey and Laidlaw focus on the social constitution of action types such as the Jain *pūjā* and argue for the arbitrary connection between ritualized actions and meaning, they nevertheless open up for the connection between ritualized actions and individual meaning through their view of ritual acts as "apprehensible" (Humphrey and Laidlaw 1994: 211). Ritual actions invite attempts at understanding and emotional response, which does not jeopardize the nature of the act which is independent of those individual mental states—that is, if the meaning thus given does not start to push the interpretation of ritual action in the direction of individual intentionality, as when the true meaning of sacrifice is seen as residing in the purpose and motives of the individual.

My focus on the "conceptually" abstract nature of the ritualization process is not meant to contradict the basic thesis of Humphrey and Laidlaw, but is a way to develop it; the actions are not merely stipulated as particular social forms of action, but the rule-following, more or less embodied or discursive in nature, is connected to a process of making the movements as abstract as possible, as not individual in character.

This gives ritualized actions their peculiar formal character; they are meant to be instantiations of an archetype, so to speak, not expressions of individuality. This is, as I see it, very much in harmony with Humphrey and Laidlaw's line of arguing. The connection with conceptual abstraction, of seeing actions governed by ritual norms and concepts as instances of the same process, however, opens up for a closer connection between meaning and ritual action. The actions are conceptualized in that they are made to conform to an abstract scheme which can be internalized either through wordless instruction and imitation or by linguistic instruction.

Before continuing with this topic, I would like to remark that the focus on ritualization espoused by Bell, Humphrey, and Laidlaw, combined with the notion of it having degrees, opens up for a very broad spectrum of domains for ritualization. The same process is active in military drills, religious ceremonies, golf, and the automatization of movements in manufacturing. The actions are through a commitment to a set of abstract templates separated from the individual's intention: the focus is on correct performance. The difference which, nevertheless, makes it inappropriate to label all such actions as rituals is located in the higher level of instrumental rationality at work in the latter two examples. The formalization of action is then done in order to achieve certain empirical goals (hole-in-one or higher productivity) and there is no sense of sacrilege when these are changed, even though for the individual it can be difficult to break a settled habitus. The golf swing and the automatic movements of the worker in the factory are, therefore, not apprehensible in quite the same way as religious actions or civil rituals as the hauling of the flag. In these contexts, ritualized actions are parts of a symbolic world which is constituted by the abstract central notions, narratives, and personalities of that particular culture or subculture. Not all ritualized actions are therefore rituals.

By the notion of apprehension, Humphrey and Laidlaw pave a way for the reconnection to their first purpose of studying the Jain pūjā, namely, symbolism. There is thus a possibility to link their theory with that put forward by the phenomenology of religion in the form presented by Mircea Eliade, even though their theory of ritual breaks with his basic idea of the inherent nature of symbolism in, for example, the snake as a lunar animal. They have by their separation of individual intention and ritual action made symbolism secondary to ritualization: instead of the other way around, when ritualization is a way of enacting symbolical under-standings. But, according to the development of the abstract nature of ritual action above, such a connection once again becomes more inti-mate, though not the same as in the symbolism of Eliade. Sacredness then becomes the elevation of a person or a thing to the abstract nature of the intersubjective cultural world. And in order to return to ordinary life, a de-abstraction, with other words, desacralization or individualiza-tion, has to take place to effectuate its re-entrance into profane life. On the other hand, a thing becomes sacred (abstract) not by acting, but by being reserved for ritual action, by being used only in a ritual way, and it becomes desacralized by lifting that restriction on its use. In this way, ritualization is the basis of sacredness and not sacredness of ritualiza-tion. Sacred carries the meaning of being set apart, abstracted from the contingent nature of everyday life, and instead being linked to a more perfect world. The sacred is in this way differentiated from the concept of the holy as it has been used within the phenomenology of religion; the holy refers to a higher degree of being (more permanent, independent of time and space, and saturated with power), which manifests itself in our finite world. Closely connected to the holy and its holiness are the feel-ings it inspires in mortal men. Thus presented, the holy clearly presup-poses the real existence of the supernatural, but in a strictly phenomeno-logical sense, it refers to the manifestation of a more powerful form of being in the finite world. The manifestation, or hierophany, is a phenom-enon of this world, but interpreted as a natural sign, transcending the less perfect order of being. Taken in this way, the conception of the holy does not presuppose the existence of a supernatural order, but focuses on human beliefs in an encounter between different levels of being. The holy is linked to the sacred, as the abstract realm has features in com-mon with the holy, but sacredness is foremost a quality of the human elevation to that level, the process of abstraction, taking away certain qualities from human actions and things, in this way rendering them conceptual.[9]

Another feature of the abstraction of human action to the intersubjective world of ideals is that it, as indicated above, comes to share place not only with ritual norms, but with moral templates, ideal figures, and exemplary narratives. The ritual thus becomes an arena in which the person comes into contact with these models of action and thought, also enabling him or her to fuse with them and in that way acquire a new character or nature. This coming together of the individual and the ideal underscores the basic social nature of ritual, as the intersubjective world of abstract actions and narratives is by definition upheld by social processes: language, teaching, discussion, reward, and punishment. The world of ideals, into which the individual enters, is in a sense the collective memory of the social group, being in need of constant reactivation and transmission to new generations (Hervieu-Léger 2000; Assmann 2006). Ritualization is a means for individuals to enter into that world, in order to handle it, serve it, and to benefit from it.

Once again the similarity with theatrical performance is close as also there the same processes are at play, actors holding up their persona to let the public engage with, for example, the template of moral and immoral love, of honor and shame. The abstract realm is acted out, perceived and felt, but in religious rituals a higher degree of seriousness is involved, a commitment entailing the notion of real transformation and not only catharsis. The theatrical performance could evolve into pure entertainment (catharsis as merely emotional activation) and would still be a performance, though of a superficial sort, while ritual as entertainment would have lost a significant part of its ritual character. The borders are of course nebulous; rituals can be more or less performance-oriented and theatre more or less ritualistic (cf. Turner 1988). Nevertheless, theat-

---

9 For a similar differentiation between the numinous and the sacred, both species of the The Holy, see Rappaport (1997: 277–405), though for him the bifurcation is based on the sacred being discursive while the numinous is ineffable (1997: 371).

rical performance builds on the distinction between actor and persona—and characteristically the audience for the most part consists of passive perceivers being less committed than in living rituals, while it is the connection with the world of intersubjective ideal entities that unites theatre and ritual.[10] If theatrical action moves toward extreme realism, it cannot, nevertheless, escape the exemplary, letting one case represent a larger set, otherwise the problem of relevance will become acute: as in the case of Andy Warhol's 8-hour long film of a man sleeping.

Ritualization in its idealization of action, promoting it to the world of abstract entities, not merely facilitates the relation between the world of ideals and that of concrete life, but for this very reason it is also of central importance for religion. Or the other way around, religion as founded on the belief in the personification of the ideal order is vital for ritual action and the maintenance of a collective world of abstract principles. Because the realm of the supernatural is precisely this abstract ideal world—encompassing moral norms, ideal persons, and basic patterns of conduct—is a supra-individual world of beings, entities, and principles more or less abstracted from human finitude. Through ritualization the human person is able to become sacred, to ascend to the perfect world, and enter into relations with the ideal. But at this point, it is important to emphasize that although the road of abstraction could lead to total transcendence, along a consequent *via negativa*, this is rarely the case when we come into contact with lived religion, and thus the focus is not merely on texts of speculative theology and metaphysics. It is this intermediate level where the ideal meets us in the form of persons and narratives which constitutes the arena of myth. A religion could, however, encompass both levels, for example, as a set of narratives of exemplary conduct and a more abstract system of ethical norms.

In order to understand the mentality behind religious ritualism it is

---

10 Rozik, however, remarks (2002: 75–76) that the opposition between participation and spectatorhood is not valid as a criterion in distinguishing between ritual and theatre, as spectatorhood is a form of participation. He localizes the decisive difference instead in the opposition between efficacy and description, or action and thinking. However, the participation characterized by action and efficacy is mostly more intense than that taking place according to description and thinking.

necessary to abstain from the nominalist impulse inherent in modernity and instead *pace* Plato emphasize that the ideal, the abstract realm, in a religious context is not seen as the pale reflection of sensual real life, forcing us to breathe the thin air of metaphysical speculation, but, on the contrary, it is embraced as the result of an ascension on the ladder of being: the higher up on the ladder, the more perfect realizations of being await us. The intersubjective cultural world is, hence, considered more objective than the changing earth, the norm more real than concrete action. Through ritualization, the human social group ascends to the level of the ideal and, this being typical of the religious impulse, tries to benefit from the richness of being found there. The holiness of a god or a goddess corresponds to its level of abstraction, and to reach the respective levels demands a similar effort of sacralization on the part of the human, or alternatively to take refuge in the idea of divine grace. The absolute being, the most abstract entity, is of course the most powerful, according to this way of reasoning. However, confronted with heights of abstraction like this, the human intellect runs out of steam and the being thus conceived transcends the power of imagination. The tendency toward personification and the formulation of a mythological narrative then becomes problematic.

To be intimate with such an abstract godhead entails leaving cognition and imagination behind and is the province of the mystic, who enters the path on which everything is abstracted, finally entering into nothingness, which at the same time is the fountainhead of being and power as such.

The raising of the individual by ritualization into the abstract world makes the question of individuation topical as the ritual person has become de-individuated, losing its specific personality by assuming an abstract persona, a ritual mask.[11] The question is then how the transformation back to the individual person takes place. In one sense, the prob-

---

11 When the aim of the ritual is a transformation of the person, its de-individualization can take the form of undressing. That is, the signs which connect the personal identity with the social identity are removed, and the person is invested with new signs which establishes a new social identity and at the same time facilitates its internalization, establishing also a new interior personal identity.

lem of individuation is a question of relevance, of connecting the abstract actions to the lifeworld of the individual and to that of the social group. In rituals, there is, thus, not merely a movement toward the abstract, but reality in its earthly contingent form is very much present with all its pressing demands. Not only is ritual necessary for interaction with the notional and normative elements of a culture, but it presents itself also as a remedy due to the reality of *inter alia* death, diseases, misfortune, hatred, betrayal of trust, war, scarcity of food, defamation, persecution, anxiety, depression, and injustice. These sources of pain motivate the ritual ascension of man, the search for contact with the holy, in order to overcome, or at least to be able to handle, evils such as death.

In a second sense, besides relevance, individuation is literally a question of becoming an individual once more, because if a person cannot leave its abstract character achieved by ritualization, he or she has, in principle, to continue to live like a personification of a norm—something which, on the other hand, could be a goal through a strategy of hyper-ritualization, a process in which increasingly more details of life are ritualized, not only governed by moral norms indicating the goodness or badness of actions, but ritual norms actually controlling the precise performance of the actions. Individuality is then deferred to the margins of life, to those areas where there is still room of maneuver for instrumental reasoning and action. In order to make profane life possible, the individual has to return to the level of the concrete going through a process of individuation, thereby shedding the extraordinary abstract state into which the individual had entered. However, the person leaves the ritual transformed, with the semiosis leaving traces: if abstraction is the ascendance to the level of form partially leaving matter behind, a modified form re-enters into matter, and a different person exits the ritual. The ritual functions as the fire of the goldsmith; it makes the material pliable to adopt a new form which when cooled preserves this new identity. The final ritual of the Vedic soma sacrifice was, for example, a bath, and in Hinduism water has *inter alia* this cooling effect, besides that of cleansing and removing "the sacral state."

The contact with the ideal order of a culture is a way of tapping resources of being and power, at the same time as the world of ideals is upheld: the gods both give boons and are in need of the sacrificial food. And it is precisely on the ritual ground that the social and personal identity of the individual is made, and consequently moral-legal personhood conferred, weaving the web of interpersonal relations; and in all this the semiotic processes taking place on the surface of the person are of central importance.[12] The ritual person in its abstract state is placed in the ideal world which is enacted in the ritual setting, and the abstraction of individuality makes it possible for the individual to enter into contact with the ideal entities: gods, norms (e.g. the divine law), social roles (the king), and notions (wisdom). As ritualization entails some degree of disembodiment, the individual becomes in a sense conceptual and liable to manipulation in the manner of concepts, thus taking on signification in a radical way. Analogy, hence, works in the manner of identification: water cleanses in this state in a much more profound and radical way than ordinary water. However, in order for the water to be able to do this, it must also have been rendered abstract through sacralization; sacred water is not ordinary water; it is conceptual water on the level of the ideal. In light of this, we can understand the viewpoint of pious Hindus desir-

---

12 The different levels of individuality, social identity, personality, and universal concept come together in the fascinating theme of personal names. These hover ambiguously between the pure reference of e.g. "Andrew" as a label affixed to a particular man and "Andrew Smith" as indicating inclusion in a family (or social group), however vague, and Andrew as a concept signaling manliness (the etymological sense). The name can then have as one of its "meanings" the unique essence of the person, but as language operates by means of concepts which are general, this unique constitution can only be comprehended as the participation in certain general qualities, or as having only reference, a mere arrow pointing toward the interior "hidden" kernel of the personality. Such a pure reference can then be seen as participating in that essence instead of describing it through general concepts, thus taking on a partial identity with what it signifies, which cannot be linguistically expressed in any other way. The disclosure of one's true "name" is, therefore, an act of externalization which renders the person vulnerable: the individual is in a sense turned inside out. For the exploration of naming in an anthropological context, see Bruck and Bodenhorn 2006. One problem which can arise in a religious context has to do with all the Andrews: are they one person, or do they share basic characteristics participating in Andrewness, or are names only nomina? In philosophy, these problems are discussed under the heading of "proper names," which have given modern philosophers much headache, see e.g. Zink 1963 and Stroll 1998; the decisive point being precisely the tension between reference and meaning (e.g. Makin 2000 on the theories of Russell and Frege).

ing purification by bathing in the Ganges, although from a concrete perspective the river is intensely polluted (Alley 2002).

RITUALIZATION AND DISCOURSE

The symbolic, conceptual nature of ritual action and ritual utensils seems to lend itself to a narrative or discursive logic, but ritualization undermines such tendencies. In a ritual, discourse can become ritualized, entailing a double process of movement away from individual intention. First, as described by Ricoeur, instead of being discourse in the meaning of a message formulated at a specific time and in a certain context, texts are fixed, for example by inscription or orally through memorization (cf. the Vedic traditions). A prayer written down, for example the Our Father, then becomes in principle disconnected from the original context and the intention of the author, and for 2000 years an almost infinite variety of worlds have been opened up in front of it, to use the parlance of Ricoeur. However, a prayer can move away from intentionality in a second step, in that it is ritualized. This means that it should be performed in accordance with a norm, leading to the prayer taking on a norm-like character. The focus is then shifted from appropriation, of understanding the prayer, toward the correct way to say it, to act it. In this process, the conceptual meaning and discursive fabric of the prayer ultimately vanish. We find here an interesting movement from *parole* to *langue*. The spoken utterance (*parole*) is elevated to the synchronic normative structure of language, that is, *langue*. But as rules of grammar lack semantic content, the prayer becomes in this way meaningless, or, perhaps more correctly, the meanings of the words become secondary to the aspect of correct performance. In the ritual context, discourse if ritualized to a high degree becomes then an enactment of the rules for ritual utterance. It is, therefore, of no consequence that neither the participants nor even the priest or magician himself understand the archaic language used, or formulas which when transposed into the discursive mode lack semantic value altogether. A favorite example of Frits Staal is Vedic mantras changed beyond recognition through the insertion of vowels.

Ritualization consequently makes the use of discourse *qua* discourse difficult in a ritual setting. In the ritual proceedings, the logic of the sign is more that of a room full of concepts acting upon each other. It is an eminently practical situation, as it is an enactment of ideal notions, persons, and entities; it is the logic of action, but carried out on a conceptual level. Ritual action has a chronological structure as a narrative, but a narrative is mostly constructed according to the intentions of characters, how they clash, become frustrated, and finally fulfilled (comedy) or left eternally unsatisfied (tragedy).[13] Ritual in giving up individual intention, though not obliterating it, cannot easily be structured in this way, because ritual performers try to act in accordance with the norms, to embody the ideal. In that sense, they can personify ideal virtues and motives as hatred and obedience, the god versus the demon, thereby moving toward the logic of theatrical performance. Ritualization, however, at least when taken to its extreme, de-emphasizes through its normative aspect the narrative dimension. Rituals also allow several threads of action to go on at the same time, something which is toilsome to achieve in a narrative. This makes a neat cause and effect structure lined out in time more complicated to achieve in a ritual—although this is perhaps not always neccesarily a goal.

When one really wants to experience genuine discursive moments in a ritual, either a non-ritual space has to be created, as with the Christian sermon, or a ritual segment can be very slightly ritualized, in order to allow space for the discursive logic, such as the readings upon which the sermon comments. Notwithstanding, in the case of reading from scripture, it is more difficult to uphold the discursive nature than in preaching, as ritualization still exercises great influence. For example, the reading is opened and ended with formulas, which are thus similar to ritual greetings and adieus; it is common that the reader adopts a manner of reading which is archaic, that is, ritualized, done according to the norm. Or one could pronounce the text in a "correct" way, a more formal, norm-like way of stress and tone, etc. And if regular new translations of the biblical

---

13 However, tragedy must not necessarily have a sad ending, cf. Whitmore 1919. The blending of the two genres can be seen in tragi-comedy (Dunn 1996: 158; Wallace 2007: 55–57).

texts are not offered, the semantic dimension gradually slips away. We can understand the great unwillingness on the part of some people when new translations are introduced; it is basically a conflict between a ritualized and discursive viewpoint. The protestant emphasis on discourse has also in some denominations led to deritualization and to an anti-ritual ideology.[14] In that context, internalization is basically modeled on the process of understanding. The ideal entities presented in the form of discourse are made interior by understanding and finally anchored in the soul through an act of faith.

RITUAL ACTION SEMIOTICS

Ritualization opens up an avenue for internalization which differs from teaching in that it does not in principle depend on understanding, but on the efficacy of action. It is a form of semiotic action as indicated by speech act theory which focuses on discourse as actions, for example the formula "Hereby I pronounce you man and wife."[15] Ritual action, though bearing testimony to the same union of language and action, approaches this from the opposite direction: it is action functioning in the manner of language. The speech act is an utterance which truly functions as an action, in that it brings about change, while the "act speech" is an act which functions as language without distancing itself from the aspect of causality as discourse has done. For example, if hitting a person in the face first has as its object to render the opponent unconscious, but later evolving into a sign of enmity, it could in a third step, in analogy to a speech act ("I declare you my enemy"), actually make a person your enemy—with the formalized act functioning as a means of communication. As a ritual act, however, the ritual slapping can retain the primary aspect of efficient causality, namely the effect of rendering the opponent senseless, but this is now being achieved on a semiotic level. The slapping of the abstract notion of the enemy as represented in, for example, a statue is then not merely a way of openly declaring another group as

14 Complete deritualization is nevertheless very hard to achieve. Cf. the ritualism controversy in Anglicanism during the nineteenth century (Yates 1999).
15 For a recent edited work on this, see Vanderveken and Kubo 2001.

the enemy, but could involve the idea of actually hurting the enemy. This is what has been labeled as magical thinking, the origin and nature of which, especially its rationality or lack thereof, has puzzled scholars.[16] According to the theoretical perspective elaborated here, this form of action, effected according to a special logic of meaning and often characterized as magical, is also natural to religious ritual, when the ideal world is taken as having a reality of its own. It is more a question of ritual thinking than a special magical mindset. For when matter is abstracted, analogy becomes the same as partial identity, and in the ideal world, identical twins are in fact only one person, making them conceptually ambiguous: being two and one at the same time.

A perfect copy cannot exist on this level, because it cannot by any criteria be distinguished from the original. Two notions having the same characteristics are, like the twins, actually one notion and can only be individuated through being thought by different embodied minds. Disembodied minds would by thinking the same thought acquire partial identity. Naturally, the implications of this become evident first in a more intellectual religious tradition, as found in the Vedic brāhmaṇas, but also on lower levels of abstraction the same tendency can be witnessed.

A feature of the special action semiotics of ritualized action, however, points to a dilemma at the heart of ritual practice, namely that actions do not directly refer to any symbolical value, for example concepts such as purity or salvation; they instead refer to the norms regulating the action. When an action is ritualized, it is made to conform to the ritual norm in such a way as to abstract away idiosyncrasies as much as possible—the person tries to become like the norm and not merely to follow it. In this way, the person is subjected to a semiotic process, but the person does not acquire what is usually called symbolical meaning, as the norm is a statement on how to act, not the "meaning" of the act. To ritualize an action is, on the one hand, to render it meaningless—it is divorced from the intention of the individual—but, on the other hand, this is a process of signification and thus also of meaning, with the meaning acquired

---

16 See e.g. the cognitive theory of Jesper Sørensen (2006).

being that of a norm. The foundational semantic double nature of ritualization is provided by the tension between, on the one hand, the disconnecting of action from individual intentionality, connecting it instead to
the meaning of the ritual norm, in this way achieving a focus on correct performance. And, on the other hand, ritualization allows action to
become semiotic, being able to act upon other abstract entities and in its
turn being acted upon by them, all according to the special logic of ritual
semiotics. Action becoming ritualized thus loses its meaning and at the
same time becomes meaning.

CHAPTER TWO

Interiorization

A primary task that confronts the person wanting to write about ritual interiorization is that the concept of interiorization contains many different meanings. A fact which prompted Yael Bentor, in his article "Interiorized Fire Rituals in India and in Tibet," to write:

> The term "interiorization" may pertain to a mental performance of the ritual, to the replacement of the ritual with a continuous process of life such as breathing or eating, to a particular way of life such as renunciation, to an actual performance with an inner interpretation, to the replacement of the external ritual with an internal one, and so forth. (2000: 596)

But, to complicate things further, it is not only rituals and other rule-governed activities that show traces of interiorization processes—interiorization could also be used as a principle in the interpretation of, for example, myths.[17] We therefore meet the word interiorization in many disciplines, as in medicine and sociology, where it carries quite different meanings, although they are based on the same fundamental metaphor. In investigations of concrete religious phenomena that involve interiorization, different concepts are also used: internalization, interiorization, psychologization, subjectivization, or spiritualization;[18] and the same word sometimes carry different meanings in the hands of various scholars.

This is not an uncommon situation facing the theoretical laborer in

---

17 See e.g. Jonas 1969 on the interiorization of the heavenly ascent in Gnosticism. The ritual enactment is also discussed.

18 For an equation of interiorization with spiritualization in the context of Ezekiel's vision of the throne-chariot see Launderville 2004: 363.

the field of religion, where the student is often tempted to despair when having to acknowledge that central notions such as religion, ritual, and myth seem to stubbornly resist all attempts at definition, and that no consensus can be achieved. The terminological confusion, nevertheless, points to a need for definition and clarification, but also, and more profoundly, indicates a lack of common theoretical ground.

Several different notions are as already mentioned used in the scholarly literature for denoting the phenomena that are here referred to as instances of ritual interiorization, but these notions also cover other processes not to be confused with the more specialized meaning I am trying to demarcate. In the following, the similarities and divergences between the concepts of internalization, spiritualization, and interiorization will, therefore, be delineated, making it possible in a later stage to elaborate on, for example, the relation between ritual interiorization and internalization.

INTERNALIZATION AND EXTERNALIZATION

As is immediately apparent, both interiorization and internalization refer to the basic process of making something inner, or of aligning something to the interior, to what is internal.[19] The two words are, therefore, sometimes used interchangeably, but internalization has acquired a prominent use within sociology, signifying the process an individual undergoes when taking certain norms, values, and attitudes as stable points of departure for his or her actions, for example that one should remove one's shoes before entering a temple or that it is wrong to eat meat.[20] T. Z. Lavine in his article "Internalization, Socialization, and Dialectic" writes:

19 Everywhere there is a movement from an exterior to an interior, internalization or interiorization can be used in a more or less technical sense. Interiorization, for example, is used as a term in literary theory denoting techniques for revealing the inner psychological life of the characters (Dorward 1985). For a use of internalization in the same meaning, see McKeon 2000: 485ff.

20 For an attempt to describe the internalization of norms from a behavioristic perspective, influenced by George Herbert Mead and polemizing against the position of Talcott Parsons, see Scott 1971; cf. Campbell (1964: 392) who takes interiorization and introjection as synonyms of internalization (of norms).

In current usage in contemporary social science to internalize a normative element of one's society is to render it a (relatively) stable and enduring structure within the inner life of the individual. (1981: 92)

Lavine, however, emphasizes that this social internalization, that is, socialization, is derived from the psychological notion of internalization, more precisely Freud's oedipal internalization, from which it significantly differs.[21] It is especially the conflictual elements of psychological internalization that, according to him, have faded away as the "conflict relationship between libidinal and aggressive impulses" (1981: 93), and the result is an idealized perfectly socialized individual. The conflict, or tension, here displayed between a sociological functionalist perspective and a psychological psychoanalytic one is perhaps due to the concept of internalization highlighting the borderline between the psychological and the social—the liminal zone between the outer and inner—in that it points to a process that moves from exteriority to interiority, thereby connecting these domains. In such a situation, the psychologist naturally wants to elaborate on the complexity of the inner, in order not to be superseded by a simple projection, of for example norms, from the social to the psychological realm. And, vice versa, a sociological theory cannot elaborate too much on intrapsychical mechanisms involved in socialization, as this would defer the focus from the social to the psychological. The optimum, therefore, seems to be a theory which could deal both with the psychic and the social realm, or smoothly incorporate the approaches of psychology and sociology within a larger framework; but the problem will remain, that is, whether it is psychology or sociology that should take precedence in such an integration, as seen in the opening lines of S. Stryker's article on social psychology in the *International Encyclopedia of the Social & Behavioral Sciences*:

---

21 The concept of interiorization has also been introduced within psychoanalysis as a technical term for the patient's interiorization of analytical dialogue. Moshe Spero (1999: 172), however, alternatively uses the notions of internalization and interiorization in discussing this phenomenon. For an attempt to clarify the taxonomy of internalization in a Freudian context, and thus dealing with concepts such as introjection, imitation, identification, and incorporation, see Schafer 1968.

In practice, there are two social psychologies. Psychological social psychology assumes that "in the beginning there is the individual" and focuses on individuals' social cognitions. Sociological social psychology assumes that "in the beginning there is society"; its distinguishing charge is to locate interactional processes in their social structural context. This difference leads to differences in problems studied, conceptualizations of problems, and research findings. (Stryker 2001: 14409)

At this point, the basic ontology of critical realism as presented within British sociology is helpful as it recognizes the *sui generis* character of mental life and tries to resist sociological imperialism, the individual as "society's being." The following quotation from Margaret Archer's book *Being Human: The Problem of Agency* functions as a programmatic declaration giving each level some autonomy while at the same time underscoring their interdependence and causal interaction:

The properties and powers of the human being are neither seen as *pregiven*, nor as *socially appropriated*, but rather these are emergent from our relations with our environment. As such, they have relative autonomy from biology and society alike, and causal powers to modify both of them. In fact, the stratified view of humanity advocated here sees human beings as constituted by a variety of strata. Each stratum is emergent from, but irreducible to, lower levels because all strata possess their own *sui generis* properties and powers. Thus, schematically, mind is emergent from neurological matter, consciousness from mind, selfhood from consciousness, personal identity from selfhood, and social agency from personal identity. (Archer 2000: 87)

It is, furthermore, of importance to note that internalization in a psychological context is not merely the internalization of norms for behavior, but that it refers to the very establishment of a psychological inner sphere, as Eric Werner states:

In the process of internalization whole blocks of personality are integrated into the self. These blocks consist of state information (beliefs), strategic information (intentions, goals) and evaluative information (wants, wishes, emotional reactions). What happens is an internal change. (Werner 2000: 266; cf. Wallis and Poulten 2001; Millet 1978)

Ritual internalization through its role in building up and designing the individual psyche participates also in the formation of individual identity. Roy Rappaport, for example, points to the relation between ritual practice and the internalization of Jewish distinctiveness:

The high frequency of the ritual performance of Orthodox Jews not only gives frequent expression to their cultural distinctiveness, but may well cause participants to internalize that distinctiveness. This internalization has been of central importance in preserving the identity of the Jews in alien environments through the eighty or so generations that have lived and died since Titus took Jerusalem. (Rappaport 1999: 204)

Due to the important function played by internalization, it is important to differentiate it from the concept of interiorization in a ritual context. The notion of ritual interiorization is, therefore, here defined as signifying an emphasis on the inner aspects (material or mental) of a ritual action, while internalization denotes the assimilation of norms for (ritual) action; making the norm part of the interior rule book of the person.[22] Internalization, in distinction to interiorization, directs our attention to the learning of the rules governing ritual, not merely as the memorization of multiplication tables, but also as a mode of being, a

22 In some contexts, the demarcation line between these two senses (internalization and interiorization) tends to become blurred. Cf. Gade 2002, with a theoretical discussion and a case study (Qur'anic recitation) and Kugle 2003; see furthermore Bisschops 1999 and Cavallin 2003 for the use of ritual internalization in the sense of ritual interiorization (in the sense stipulated above). Furthermore, these two processes (internalization and interiorization) can be part of the same ritual practice, as indicated by Gavin Flood (2002) in his discussion of the tantric ritual of the purification of the body.

form of practice, that is, ritual in the process of becoming an integral part of the human person, as internal to the individual. Internalization, furthermore, does not in the same way emphasize the hidden nature of the interior, but focuses on something becoming an integral part of the system, as in this case, the psychosomatic unity of the human person.

Interiorization is thus reserved for designating the inclination toward the physically and mentally interior in ritual practice and discourse, but such processes obviously presuppose the internalization of the rules of ritual, attitudes, and values. At the same time, the relation between these two forms of movement toward the inner is not always without tensions, as we shall see later on.

As internalization denotes the appropriation of ritual norms, externalization in a ritual context primarily refers to the formulation of such norms. In a wider sense, however, externalization is the opposite process of socialization, referring to all those acts in which individuals express themselves, not always in an original way, but mostly as the result of previous acts of internalization, as Eric Werner writes:

> Externalization can be viewed as a complementary psychodynamic process to internalization. The externalization process takes a given representational strategic state and projects it onto the other. Yet, it is more than just projection since the actual control strategies of the self are modified. In the case of the child, the child goes into an earlier mode of behavior by externalizing functions it has previously mastered and internalized. (Werner 2000: 270)

Both internalization and externalization are, furthermore, notions signifying more than just the formulation and learning of ritual rules; they cover a wider field comprising feelings, attitudes, values, etc.—with other words, the whole spectrum of the intersubjective social and cultural world. To emphasize this relative autonomy of the social world, Peter Berger and Thomas Luckmann in *The Social Construction of Reality* (1967 [1966]) introduced a notional triad, viz. externalization, objectivation, and internalization (e.g. Berger and Luckmann 1967 [1966]: 149).

Objectivation here signifies the process wherewith human interaction becomes institutionalized and takes on a life of its own, more or less independent of the individual considered in isolation.[23] In critical realist terminology, it becomes an emergent entity (morphogenesis).

In a ritual context, externalization consequently denotes, in a first step, the actual performance in which the actors enact their internalized ritual norms, but, at the same time, through externalization the actors become involved in the application, reinterpretation, and changing of these norms—in the objectivation of ritual activity. On the discourse level, similar processes are active in the externalization of norms in manuals, in the discussion of them in ritual theology or simply the description of their performance. The internalization/externalization conceptual pair in this way makes us attentive to ritual learning and change. The interior is, on the one hand, the matrix of norms, providing templates and impulses for ritual acting and, on the other hand, the receiver of norms, attitudes, and values.

SPIRITUALIZATION AND MATERIALIZATION

At first glance, spiritualization could, as internalization, appear to be synonymous with interiorization, but at closer inspection spiritualization and interiorization emerge as overlapping but distinct notions. The affinity between the concepts is due to spiritualization denoting a movement from the material to the spiritual, and as the spiritual most commonly is viewed as beyond the scope of the human senses, an entity made spiritual acquires an inner, that is, a hidden, character, at least in relation to human persons. A form of ritual spiritualization is, for example, present in narratives describing the ritual activity of the gods, one of the many possible species of spirits (Patton 2009). In that context, spiritualization implies that human ritual actors have been exchanged for spirits,

---

23 Objectivation is already presented by Berger in an earlier article written together with Stanley Pullberg (1965). There it is explicitly derived from the Marxist notion of reification though not synonymous with it. The process is described as going from objectivation to objectification through alienation to reification. For a critique of the Marxist version of reification and the reformulation of it (together with objectivation) by Berger and Luckmann, see Pitkin (1987).

who perform a spiritual—or at least a cosmic or superhuman—ritual; for it is not certain that such a divine liturgy is construed as directed to spiritual effects, as indicated in the following interior monologue of Prajāpati, the creator god par excellence in the Vedic *brāhmaṇa* texts:

> In the beginning Prajāpati, being desirous of offspring, sacrificed with this sacrifice: "May I abound in offspring and cattle; may I obtain prosperity; may I become glorious; may I become an eater of food!" so he thought. (Eggeling 1966: part 1, 375)

This example lends itself most easily to an analysis as a paradigmatic ritual performance of which human ritual acts are imitations, in that way partaking of its primordial power. However, I would like to draw the analytical focus to the narrative at the same time constituting a displacement of a human ritual to a spiritual sphere, even if this does not imply the abolishment of the concrete ritual, but provides a superhuman foundation for it.

Besides the displacement of a whole ritual to the spiritual plane, the liturgy could be spiritualized merely to a certain extent and not in its entirety. That is, if a religious tradition embraces the idea of one or more souls somehow united with the human body, then spiritualization can signify some of the same processes as the notion of ritual interiorization covers; turning the ritual toward the inner and spiritual part(s) of the human person. Such a spiritualization of a ritual is often closely connected to symbolical and allegorical methods of interpretation, which *inter alia* can be applied to rituals, but also to other domains such as myths, precepts, and actions in general. In Christian exegetical discourse, Origen championed such an allegorical or spiritual reading of biblical texts, in an effort to uncover the spiritual gospel lying behind the textual gospels:

> [S]o also the gospel, which is thought to be understood by all who read it, teaches a shadow of the mysteries of Christ. And that which John calls an eternal gospel, which would properly be called a spiritual gos-

pel, clearly presents both the mysteries presented by Christ's words and the things of which his acts were symbols, to those who consider "all things face to face" concerning the Son of God himself. (Origen 1989: 42)

This spiritualizing exegetical strategy ("exegetical gymnastics," Clarke 2003: 33, or "a mode of eucharistic performance," Dawson 2001: 65) also covers ritual, a hermeneutical approach which was already present in the New Testament due to the central question of the degree to which Jewish ritual precepts had validity in post-messianic times:

Everyone, then, in whom Christ has dwelt, worships God neither in Jerusalem nor on the mountain of the Samaritans, but because he has learned that "God is spirit," serves him spiritually "in spirit and truth," [Jn 4.24] and no longer worships the Father and creator of all things figuratively. (Origen 1989: 41)

The spiritualization of a ritual provides a tradition with a flexible notion of ritual, or, as is often the case, an extension of the most prestigious ritual form: sacrifice. Non-ritual actions can, thereby, be defined as sacrifices, assuming the prestige and merit of the sacrificial proceedings: A similar spiritualization (and extension) of the concepts "warfare" and "martyrdom" has, for example, been used in Islamic exegesis:

Just as the doctrine of jihad was spiritualized and assimilated to the internal spiritual struggle of the believer, so also the doctrine of martyrdom had its most characteristic classical expression in the spiritualization of martyrdom and its assimilation to the inward sacrifice of the believer. This tendency found its clearest expression in the distinction between a lesser and a greater jihad. The lesser jihad is a struggle against unbelievers, the greater jihad a struggle against the tendencies toward evil within the human spirit. (Brown 2002: 108)

Notwithstanding the similarities between interiorization and spiritualization, and that they are used interchangeably in many contexts, interiorization retains its spatial aspect, while spiritualization indicates a process more or less giving up spatiality—depending upon how radically transcendent the spiritual is conceptualized in a specific culture. Spiritualization is, therefore, here defined as the tendency to move from the tangibly material sphere to the realm of spirit, which can be personal (human or divine) or impersonal. Interiorization, on the other hand, focuses on the human person as having an intersubjective surface enclosing a physical and mental interiority.[24]

Spiritualization is, furthermore, often connected to deritualization, or a radical extension of ritual terminology into the domain of non-ritual actions, an issue which we will return to later (cf. Klawans 2002: 12). Interiorization is, on the other hand, not in principle a-ritualistic, but could be part of processes of deritualization.

A problem with spiritualization as a concept, hinted at above, is that it presupposes a basic notion of the spiritual, and an inner, subtle body, for example, hovers somewhat ambiguously between solid materiality and a transcendent spirituality with the latter's focus on impassibility, immovability, etc. Spiritualization as a concept consequently requires a cross-cultural definition of spirit, which in its turn has to be contrasted with the degree of transcendence formulated and acted upon in the specific culture studied.[25] Moreover, for the most part, we do not meet only one type of spirit, but a whole spectrum of spirits ranging from the almost

---

24 Spiritualization is not only used as denoting allegorical interpretations of myths and rituals, but also as signifying the transformation into spirit, which when applied to human persons sometimes denotes a change into a more mature spiritual state in which the spirit has assumed the highest position, a condition which rhetorically could be contrasted with the state of more earthly, worldly, or fleshly minded people. However, besides the realization of spiritual potentialities, spiritualization can refer to the actual transformation into spirit, as in the notion of a spiritual body. In the following description of platonic influences on Augustine, spiritualization carries this latter meaning: "Immediately after his conversion, Augustine of Hippo (354–430 A.D.) found the idea of salvation through "angelization" attractive. An angelized version of salvation envisaged the eventual elimination of the body by its total spiritualization. With time, however, he learned as a Christian to recognize more positive value in physical creation" (Gelpi 2001: 128).

25 E.g. in the *Encyclopedia of Religion* under the entry "Spirit" (1987: vol. 14: 11), there are only references to other articles, but no separate article: "*For discussion of the difference between spirit and soul, see Soul, especially articles on Greek and Hellenistic concepts and Christian Concept.*"

material, or thinly material, as ghosts, to the wholly transcendent, for example some form of philosophical Supreme Being. What kind of spirit one chooses as reference point for the notion of spiritualization is, therefore, of importance for its value as a tool in comparative analyses. One strategy which is used within the cognitive study of religion is, then, to replace "spiritual" with other more precise notions such as contra-intuitive, supernatural, or superhuman and thus eschew spiritualization in favor of expressions such as a higher degree of contra-intuitiveness (e.g. Boyer 1994).

The opposite process of spiritualization is naturally materialization which moves toward the concrete from the abstract, from the spiritual toward the material. As spiritualization, but contrary to the notion of exteriorization and externalization, materialization does not build upon the interior/exterior divide, and, therefore, does not easily fit into a model with interiorization; but it is, nevertheless, worth mentioning in this context, as it can be used to describe aspects connected to, or partly overlapping with, externalizing or exteriorizing processes. If the interior is conceptualized as mainly spiritual or mental, then the utterance of ritual formulas could be interpreted as a manifestation of the nonmaterial in the material; coming close in meaning to Eliade's notion of hierophany, the manifestation of the holy: "a reality of an entirely different order than those of this world becomes manifest in an object that is part of the natural of profane sphere" (Eliade and Sullivan 1987: 313; cf. Orsi 2005: 77).

To some extent materialization is thus synonymous with externalization and objectivation, but it often retains the meaning of an agent not only expressing itself in matter, but actually creating matter in the very act of expression (cf. Keller 2002: 40; Barker and Galasiński 2001: 49). As the latter meaning transcends the ontological agnosticism presupposed by religious studies, the notion of materialization, as spiritualization, is here used not to refer to actual movements from the spiritual to the material, but to discursive strategies delineating and emphasizing such processes. For example, in the case of the Indian Mahaguru Satya Sai Baba, a conspicuous feature of his performances (darśan) was the alleged materialization of objects, for example through vomiting forth little *liṅgas*, something which affirms his divine nature, as he is believed to have been the incarnation of both Shiva and Shakti (Palmer 2005).

INTERIORIZATION OF RITUAL EFFICACY

After the definition of interiorization in relation to internalization and spiritualization, we can move on to tackle the question of the different types of interiorization since there are various parts or aspects of ritual activity that can be interiorized, a fact which points to the need for a more detailed taxonomy of interiorization. In the following, the first step in that direction will be to demarcate three aspects of rituals which can be interiorized, and then to proceed with the description of subcategories under these broad aspects of ritual.

The first category is made up of interiorization, which entails that the efficacy of the ritual is interiorized, that is, the efficacy is considered as dependent on some inner quality for functioning properly. This is, for example, the case in the biblical emphasis on the moral goodness of the person bringing an offering or sacrifice to God. In order for the sacrifice to achieve its aim, it must be acceptable to God and hence be accompanied by upright intentions. The opposite position considers the efficacy of the ritual as independent of the moral intentions and status of the ritual participants, and instead as linked to the exact performance of all the ritual details.

Besides efficacy, the actual ritual performance can be interiorized, as when a sacrifice is performed partially or totally in the mind. It is not necessary that the efficacy of such a mental ritual is dependent upon the moral quality of the performer, but ritual efficacy could instead be considered as dependent on the performer managing to execute some complicated visualizations according to established norms.

The third aspect that will be considered is the effects of the ritual; because even if the efficacy is considered as linked to the moral quality of the performer and the ritual performance consists of complicated visualizations, the purpose could be external, as to heal a blind eye or to increase the wealth of the ritual sponsor. If, on the other hand, also the effect is interiorized, then it could be presented as spiritual progress, illumination, or the strengthening of some particular virtue.

The above categorization of ritual into three aspects (efficacy, performance, and effects) is not put forward as constituting an exhaustive mapping of all possible aspects of ritual activity; it is foremost an attempt to create a relevant taxonomy for the discussion of interiorization. The aspects have not been chosen according to a specific ontology of ritual actions, but for their pragmatic value. It is, therefore, possible and recommendable to add ritual aspects that can be interiorized when analyzing specific cases, in this way enlarging and modifying the model. Anticipating this process somewhat and thus increasing the usefulness of the three aspects chosen here, they will be made more concrete and nuanced by the introduction of some subdivisions. We thus descend one step on the ladder of abstraction, drawing nearer to the level of actual cases of interiorization. This will hopefully facilitate the analytical work of the reader who becomes inspired to commence an investigation of ritual interiorization in a concrete tradition. But, I emphasize, it should not be taken as a rigid scheme, it is offered as reflections on aspects of ritual practice and discourse that can be involved in processes of interiorization.

The category which deals with the efficacy of the ritual acts is in the following divided into types that make alternatively interior purity, bodily condition, feelings, knowledge, spiritual qualities, or intentionality the prerequisites for ritual efficacy.[26] These can of course be combined and an especially tight connection can be expected to exist between intentionality and moral purity, but such a link is not inevitable. A person could, for example, have a morally good intention at a particular

---

26 The division of mental interiority into different subcategories as intentionality, gnosis, or feelings is, basically, dependent on a relevant categorization of mental life, and ultimately on a psychological theory. A psychoanalytical approach to ritual interiorization could take as its basic categories the notions of id, ego, and superego, for example. The categories chosen here do not therefore constitute an exhaustive enumeration of all possible types of interiorization. We can, for example, bring in other mental faculties as the memory or imagination, but the categories presented above are chosen on the principle of relevance, but, as already mentioned, they constitute a fallible first attempt at systematization.

ritual performance, but, at the same time, be considered impure due to a previous defilement, and hence his sacrifice or offering is rejected as inefficacious or outright obnoxious. The concept of ritual purity prevalent in a tradition can also be modeled on physical dirtiness or sickness, rather than on intentional evil.[27] The nature of impurity is in such cases partially independent of conscious ethical choices, and could, for example, be the result of an unlawful action unknowingly performed, as when Oedipus married his mother, or the consequence of having merely touched an unclean object, as a dead body. An example of the latter case is given in one of the rules of Leviticus, emphasizing that impurity makes a person ritually ineligible:

> But those who eat flesh from the Lord's sacrifice of well-being while in a state of uncleanness shall be cut off from their kin. When any one of you touches any unclean thing—human uncleanness or an unclean animal or any unclean creature—and then eats flesh from the Lord's sacrifice of well-being you shall be cut off from your kin. (Lev. 7.20–21)[28]

In ancient Judaism, impurity was thus a broad category not only denoting the consequences of intentional evil—which has, for example, prompted Jonathan Klawans (2000: 22–42) to make a distinction between moral and ritual purity. Therefore, in the context of interiorization, impurity has to be interpreted as a very broad category comprising all cases of inner impurity in distinction to exterior impurities such as leprosy, but

---

27 One could argue that we are actually dealing with the metaphorical interconnections between two conceptual dichotomies: purity and impurity in a physical sense, plus the contrast between good and evil. But one could also argue that both are dependent on a more basic principle contrasting order with disorder (cf. Douglas 1966). Purity is then, in the same way as goodness, closely connected to what is well ordered—with interior impurity being a hidden disorder of the person, evil in its disintegrating character. We should expect a close connection between moral and physical evil in this context. It is natural that also further dichotomies attach to impurity as social status (high–low), aesthetical (beautiful–ugly). Also these have a direct connection with the view of order contra disorder: a well ordered society and what is well proportioned.

28 See, however, Lev. 4, which allows for an atoning sacrifice if the transgression of a rule was made unintentionally.

both of these can of course be combined into the view of leprosy as the result of an unlawful act (cf. Num. 12.10). The outer impurity becomes, in that way, a sign and an effect of inner moral pollution, in Peircean terminology: an index.

The question of inner physical purity directs the attention to a wider field of bodily interiority. In principle, it is not only interior purity that could be considered as vital for the ritual to achieve its aims, but, for example, also the health or condition of the interior organs could be a *sine qua non* for a successful ritual performance. We can see such a pattern of thought in the Azande beliefs regarding the basis of witchcraft as reported by Evans-Pritchard in 1937. Witchcraft according to the Azande is based on a special inherited organ called *mangu*, which is oval in shape and situated between the breastbone and the intestines. As this source of witchcraft is physically interior there are two methods of gaining knowledge of it, either through some form of divination or through an autopsy after the death of the supposed witch. However, the Azande differentiate between witchcraft and sorcery, the latter being the ritualistic variant which works through spells and medicines, while the former is a power of which the person equipped with a *mangu* could even be unaware (cf. Turner 1994 [1967]: 118). Perhaps this is typical since it is very difficult even for the individual to ascertain the presence of an interior physical condition, and we should instead expect a blend of physical and psychical elements as in the manipulation of inner energy in tantric yoga (e.g. Flood 2006: 146–70).

Besides inner purity, whether ethical or not, rituals could be believed to draw their efficacy chiefly from feelings and moods such as peace, ecstasy, happiness, or pain. These feelings must then be present in order for the ritual to achieve its stipulated goal, which can also be a feeling, or a form of spiritual catharsis: finding the way to one's true self. One example of this is ritualized laughter, which, for example, the late guru Bhagwan Shree Rajneesh (1931–1990), the founder of the Osho-Rajneesh movement, advocated:

I have chosen one of my therapists to create a new meditative therapy.

The first part will be Yaa-Hoo!—for three hours, people simply laugh for no reason at all. And whenever their laughter starts dying they again say, "Yaa-Hoo!" and it will come back. Digging for three hours you will be surprised how many layers of dust have gathered upon your being. It will cut them like a sword, in one blow. For seven days continuously, three hours every day ... you cannot conceive how much transformation can come to your being.

And then the second part is "Yaa-Boo." The first part removes everything that hinders your laughter—all the inhibitions of past humanity, all the repressions. It cuts them away. It brings a new space within you, but still you have to go a few steps more to reach the temple of your being, because you have suppressed so much sadness, so much despair, so much anxiety, so many tears—they are all there, covering you and destroying your beauty, your grace, your joy. (Osho 2005)

One problem which we encounter in such cases is that feelings are both interior (feeling of pain) and exterior (manifest pain behavior), and if they are interiorized, that is, when the subjective dimension is emphasized, then the hidden character of the interior makes it difficult to decide if the ritual was successful; it becomes primarily the responsibility of each participant to guarantee and estimate the success of the ritual. On the other hand, feelings could be increasingly ritualized so what is required is not the actual feeling of peace, but the ritualized peaceful gestures, or stereotyped ritual mourning. In the example above, this would entail that the three hours of ritualized laughter were not necessarily accompanied by any particular subjective feeling. An emphasis on feelings as prerequisites for ritual efficacy can thus move in an interiorizing direction, but this stress on the inner can as easily be externally regulated, as when the actual feeling is not in focus, but the enactment of it, or when one becomes occupied with exterior signs, for example laughter as a sign that the person is really feeling happy. This ambivalence between inner state and its outer manifestation underlies the famous thesis of Max Weber on the protestant ethic, that the inner condition of predestined salvation had to be externally manifested or enacted:

> So, wherever the doctrine of predestination was held, the question could not be suppressed whether there were any infallible criteria by which membership in the electi could be known. (Weber 2001: 66)

> Thus, however useless good works might be as a means of attaining salvation, for even the elect remain beings of the flesh, and everything they do falls infinitely short of divine standards, nevertheless, they are indispensable as a sign of election. (Weber 2001: 69)

Another example of when feelings are seen as important in a ritual context is when an initiand in a rite of passage is compelled to undergo ordeals which involve as their main ingredient the feeling of pain, that is, pain becomes a prerequisite for the ritual to achieve its transformative goal. However, also in such a case, the question is to what degree we witness a ritual interiorization, an emphasis on the subjective feeling of pain, or the ritualization of pain, as Alan Morinis writes:

> I make the assumption that initiands actually feel the intense pain that appears to be inflicted on them. This cornerstone of my concerns must remain as assumption because we cannot gain access to the inner experience of those who are undergoing what appears to an observer as an ordeal. (Morinis 1985: 164, cf. Glucklich 2001: 133)

In the same way as feelings can be considered necessary for the efficacy of a ritual act, knowledge could be deemed indispensable. The rituals are then considered as invalid if an ignoramus has performed them—only an enlightened or duly educated ritual officiator is qualified. The same principle at work in interiorization with a focus on feelings applies when one makes knowledge a prerequisite for ritual efficacy, that is, how we are to know that this ritual officiator is knowledgeable. We can of course question him and by this means test the breadth and depth of his knowledge, but this will be a cumbersome process to enact for every ritual, and the wisdom of the priest is, therefore, in most cases subjected to the semiotic process which turns the interior state into a sign, with the consequence that in a second step the sign itself can become the repository of knowledge (or legitimacy, power, or charisma) and one can thus put questions directly to it. The drum of the Sami *noaidi* was, for example, inscribed with the signs of gods, animals, and objects, and when used as an instrument of divination a ring was placed upon it which moved when the drum was beaten, in this way indicating whether the hunt would be successful, in what direction the bear was to be found, etc. The drum both functioned as an instrument inducing the *noaidi* into shamanistic trance and as a cosmos of signs that could reveal the information desired by the community consulting the *noaidi* (Kjellström and Rydving 1988).

In the following quotation from the Bṛhadāraṇyaka Upaniṣad (3.1.1–2), on the other hand, the priests are probed for knowledge directly, and the traditional ordained priesthood is challenged in a ritualistic knowledge duel. It constitutes a token of the continuous shift of attention from ritual performance to knowledge within the Vedic text corpus:

Janaka, the king of Videha, once set out to perform a sacrifice at which he intended to give lavish gifts to the officiating priests. Brahmins from the Kuru and Pañcāla regions had flocked there for the occasion, and Janaka of Videha wanted to find out which of those Brahmins was the most learned in the Vedas. So he corralled a thousand cows; to the horns of each cow were tied ten pieces of gold.

He then addressed those Brahmins: "Distinguished Brahmins! Let the most learned man among you drive away these cows." But those Brahmins did not dare. So Yājñavalkya called to his pupil. "Sāmaśravas! Son, drive these cows away." And he drove them away. The Brahmins were furious and murmured: "How dare he claim to be the most learned?" (Olivelle 1998: 75–76)

This evaluation of knowledge takes place in a sacrificial context, but it contains at the same time a principle able to dislodge the whole intricate ritual system, that is, when acquaintance with the hidden meaning of the ritual acts becomes efficacious in itself.

If the categories of purity, feelings, and knowledge by now have been delineated to a sufficient degree, the category of spiritual qualities is not altogether clear. Spiritual qualities in this context are not all those that pertain to the in principle intangible aspects of the human person, which would then include purity to some degree, knowledge, and feelings. Spiritual qualities seem to constitute a residual category, signifying all the other qualities of the "soul," something which to a certain extent is true. It is, however, motivated by examples such as the priestly ordination considered as conferring a *character indelebilis* not dependent upon the moral status of the priest, but being a permanent change of the spiritual state of the priest, remaining in spite of evil actions, impurity due to more mechanical causes, and level of knowledge. We are, therefore, dealing with a category of qualities which are considered either as more permanent changes of the spiritual aspects of the person or as already built into the very constitution of it.

In some traditions, there is the idea that even pure spirits are engaged in ritual activity, and to guarantee ritual efficacy some qualities of the spirits are required, that is, not all spirits could perform the ritual in question. This is a fact which makes it necessary to speak of spiritual qualities and not only of qualities of the soul. There is, for example, such a line of argument in the book of Revelation, although the worthy one is the incarnated God and in that way not only spirit. Nevertheless, what is described is a heavenly ritual act and the lamb is the uniquely qualified person to perform the opening of the scroll, in that way breaking the seals:

I saw a mighty angel proclaiming with a loud voice. "Who is worthy to open the scroll and break its seals? And no one in heaven or on earth or under the earth was able to open the scroll or to look into it. And I began to weep bitterly because no one was found worthy to open the scroll or to look into it. The one of the elders said to me, "Do not weep. See, the Lion of the tribe of Judah, the Root of David, has conquered, so that he can open the scroll and its seven seals." Then I saw between the throne and the four living creatures and among the elders a Lamb standing as if it had been slaughtered. (Rev. 5.2–6)

These basic qualities of the soul (or spirit), which I am trying to separate into a category of their own, could in a ritual tradition be considered as hereditary or as spontaneously appearing in certain individuals (i.e. some sort of charisma), or achieved through heroic struggle (e.g. the slaughtered lamb). The recognition of such qualities could of course be connected with acknowledging high levels of knowledge, purity, and lofty feelings such as compassion or holy wrath in that very same person, but this is not necessary. We should, however, not consider these categories as absolutely independent of each other, but as partly joined, while nevertheless pointing to some distinct characteristics, which can be important for analytical purposes.

One special category which is relevant for the consideration of spiritual qualities is the prerequisite of ordination which could be seen as either a bureaucratic empowerment (hence revocable) or a spiritual transformation of the person in question. In the second sense, ordination does not fall under the heading of purity, ethical or not, because, for example, as alluded to above, in the official teaching of the Catholic Church, even a apostatized priest or bishop retains the *character indelebilis* conferred by ordination (cf. Weber 2003: 203). If the spiritual state of a priest is a prime example of a quality that can be made a starting point for the interiorization of ritual efficacy, then bureaucratic ordination is not suitable for such a process. It depends on a decision taken within a religious system and recorded on, for example, paper and is in force as long as the certificate is recognized in the system. It is thus essentially exterior. Nevertheless, in the same way as the bureaucratic empowerment, the spiritual state believed to be the effect of religious ordination has to be upheld with the help of exterior documents or signs (ring, staff, etc.) and needs to be recognized by the religious group in question. Though such a priest is dispelled from the system, that is, deprived of his function, he could be considered as retaining his priestly nature. The more distressing discussion is then whether the ordination was valid in the first place—a question vital for the recognition of the spiritual state of the ritual specialist in question, and hence for his claim to fulfill a ritual function within a certain religious system.

If we reconnect to the example of the Catholic doctrine on priesthood and ritual efficacy, it is interesting that not only the knowledge, moral state, or feelings of the priest are considered inconsequential for the validity of the Eucharist, but also deviant intentionality seems not to be enough to make a Eucharistic celebration invalid, that is, the transubstantiation is not dependent upon what the priest wants, desires, or thinks of at the moment of uttering the words of institution. This is expressed in Latin as the distinction between *ex opere operato* (from the work done) and *ex opere operantis* (from the work being done), the former denoting an action depending for its efficacy on another action already done, and the latter an action depending on the quality of the acts undertaken at that very moment. In *Summa Theologiae*, for example, Thomas Aquinas argues that the Eucharist is even more disconnected from the priest's person than the other sacraments:

> Secondly, because in the other sacraments the consecration of the matter consists only in a blessing, from which the matter consecrated derives instrumentally a spiritual power, which through the priest who is an animated instrument, can pass on to inanimate instruments. But in this sacrament the consecration of the matter consists in the miraculous change of the substance, which can only be done by God; hence the minister in performing this sacrament has no other act save the pronouncing of the words. (Aquinas 1947: 3a 78:1)

Interestingly, intentionality, however, resurfaces in the Catholic normative discourse of the Eucharist as *the intention of the Church* (cf. the ritual commitment), which is made a prerequisite for the efficacy of the ritual, as in the following quotation from the Catechism of the Catholic Church on the sacraments in general: "From the moment that a sacrament is celebrated in accordance with the intention of the Church, the power of Christ and his Spirit acts in and through it, independently of the personal holiness of the minister" (*Catechism of the Catholic Church* 1994: Part 2, section 1, art. 2, IV, 1128). This complicates matters, because if the minister is to adhere to the intention of the Church, an intentional stance of his own is required, and, thereby, contrary to expectations, the efficacy of the ritual is partly interiorized. The crucial point here is whether the intention of the Church is merely the exterior following of the ritual injunctions, the performance of the correct gestures and utterances, or if an accompanying mental act is required. In the *Catholic Encyclopedia*, for example, the first interpretation is rejected:

> The Church teaches very unequivocally that for the valid conferring of the sacraments, the minister must have the intention of doing at least what the Church does. This is laid down with great emphasis by the Council of Trent (sess. VII). The opinion once defended by such theologians as Catharinus and Salmeron that there need only be the intention to perform deliberately the external rite proper to each sacrament, and that, as long as this was true, the interior dissent of the minister from the mind of the Church would not invalidate the sacrament, no longer finds adherents. The common doctrine now is that a real internal intention to act as a minister of Christ, or to do what Christ instituted the sacraments to effect, in other words, to truly baptize, absolve, etc., is required. (Delaney 1910)

In the article several types of intentions are mentioned, and especially the distinction between actual and virtual intention is important. Actual intention is an act of the will combined with the attention of the mind (intellect), while the virtual intention is dependent upon a previous actual intention of which the result is still in power. The will is still there but not present in consciousness: "In other words, the virtual intention is not a present act of the will, but rather a power (*virtus*) come about as an effect of a former act, and now at work for the attainment of the end" (ibid.). The example given is of a man having made an actual intention of going on a journey, thinking of other things while traveling, but who still has the virtual intention of reaching his destination.[29] Thus, what is required of the priest is not an actual intention when performing the Eucharistic ritual, but a virtual one. This constitutes a way of interiorizing the efficacy (the preceding actual intention) and exteriorizing it at the same time, that is, the priest needs not to think of something special during the ritual or to make a special act of the will. However, if he would make a new actual intention contradicting the previous one, then the required virtual intention would dissolve. In that case, the ritual is considered invalid and inefficacious, but this intention is an interior act, not open to direct inspection, and the indeterminacy which adheres to the inner requires that it takes manifest form in some way or other, as stated by Fr. Robert Matheus in an article on the subject:

> In this context it might be useful to examine the question of the minimum intention required from the part of the minister to administrate validly the sacraments. Since the intention is a hidden element in the minister, somehow we must be able to discern it through the external sign of the ceremonies. We will examine the controversed theory of the exterior, or better "exteriorised intention." (Matheus 2006)

On the other hand, the *reception* of the host is thoroughly interiorized in that its efficacy is considered as dependent on the moral and spiritual state of the receiver, but also on the individual's intentional stance.[30] Furthermore, the host is physically interiorized in being swallowed and thus united with the interior body which in one sense is physical, because the accidental properties of bread undergo disintegration in the digestive process, and in another sense spiritual, the spiritualized flesh making up the substance of the host uniting with the soul. In this way, the reception of the host moves away from the public ritual to an

29 This distinction could be compared with Margaret Archer's (2007) focus on reflexivity (internal conversation) and embodied practice.
30 Cf. *The Catechism of the Catholic Church*, Part 2, section 1, art. 2, IV, 1127–1128.

individual interior moment which to a large extent is beyond the reach of ritualization. The highly exteriorized theory of transubstantiation is, thereby, balanced by an equally radical interiorization of the reception of the transubstantiated bread. In this, we can sense a tension between the demands of objective validity and individual relevance: a balance which can easily be shifted, giving more importance either to exterior rituality or interior spirituality, in this way leaving the other pole to undergo atrophy.

Interiorization which focuses on intentionality makes the disposition of the ritual practitioner decisive for the efficacy of the ritual act. And, as we above have separated out spiritual qualities from moral purity and assigned them separate categories, intentionality is a more restricted notion than that denoted by *ex opere operantis*. To achieve precision in the definition of intentionality and thereby making it useful for our purposes is, however, not altogether easy. This is because intentionality as a philosophical concept denotes a relation between consciousness and some object. Thereby, intentionality in the same way as interiorization signifies a transcendence, but in a reversed manner: If interiorization signifies the transcendence of the outer in favor of the inner, then intentionality denotes the transcendence of consciousness (*intentio*) into the intended object (*intentum*), which, however, could be immanent within the mind, as pain. Intentionality, as interiorization, defines the final point of its movement (the object; interiorization: the inner) in relation to its starting point (consciousness; interiorization: the exterior). Intentionality so broadly defined comprises all mental acts, also, for example, feelings, hence it seems expedient in a second step to delimit intentionality to mean more precisely the conscious choice of mental focus. For example, forms of interiorization that make feelings decisive for ritual efficacy have been collected in a category of their own, as feelings, for example pain, mostly present themselves as inevitable phenomena for consciousness.

The kind of intentionality I am trying to define here is a combination of consciousness and will; the mere presence of an object in consciousness is not a sufficient condition. This notion of intentionality is therefore closer to the first more commonplace definition of the two enumerated by Gillet in his book *Consciousness and Intentionality* (2001: 11):

> [T]here are two meanings commonly given to the term "intentionality". The first is "purposiveness" as in "He intentionally fouled the goalkeeper" or "His omission to warn his wife about the road works was intentional". In this usage the term reflects a degree of sophisticated and rational organization of behaviour such that one pursues a plan or desired outcome by carrying out a series of voluntary actions.

> The second sense of intentionality is ... arguably related to the first and is the sense traditionally associated with the discussion of consciousness in the phenomenological tradition. In this sense intentionality is "aboutness" or that feature of states of mind that makes it sensible to talk of them having objects.

It could, moreover, be helpful, as Rickman does in a discussion of Dilthey's hermeneutical philosophy, to differentiate between intentions and motives. Rickman argues that actions undertaken primarily for achieving some objective, and not for communication, express in a clear way the intention of the actor, that is, what he intends to bring about, what type of action he is performing; the intention in doing according to Humphrey and Laidlaw. Rickman defines the intention as "the agent's immediate goal" which is different from the motive according to which he undertakes the action (Rickman 1988: 51). The motive for an action hence needs not to coincide with the purpose for which it is undertaken, as the purpose is the desired effect of the ritual while the motive is the background factor motivating the agent to strive for the purpose. The motive of a ritual act could be to please the god of one's choice, while the purpose is to remove obstacles to its cult. The difference between motive and purpose is, therefore, not of kind but consists in degree of generality (e.g. wanting to please the god of one's choice and the act of pleasing him by the sacrifice of two doves) or causal proximity (the sacrifice leads to god being pleased). Intention places itself before the causal chain leading from the proximate effect (purpose) to the secondary effect (the goal) and it designates, as in Rickman's definition, the type of action intended to be performed. The purpose tends to be intimately connected with the intention as the action "chopping at a tree with an axe" is mostly called "felling a tree" and in that way the purpose is built into the type of action. However, as argued by Humphrey and Laidlaw, this is something which is deliberately manipulated in rituals, and the chopping with an axe at a tree could in a ritual be an expressive act with the purpose to awaken the tree spirit, but also if the connection between intention and purpose becomes obscure it could evolve into a mere formal chopping with no socially agreed upon intentional purpose or motive.

Interiorizations with a focus on intentionality often concern the individual's purpose or motive for the ritual action undertaken. It could take the form of, for example, prescribing certain motives as morally good (e.g. altruism) and others as morally bad (e.g. vainglory), with the bad making the ritual inefficacious. But also the intention in doing could become interiorized, as in the case of mentally performed rituals, or when the individuals' interior understanding of their ritual acts are considered decisive for their nature—a viewpoint that leads to an anxious questioning of whether the ritual acts have been performed at all.

As argued previously, the will is the central force behind intentionality in the context of ritual action, in contrast to more passive acts as perception or reflection. For the phenomenological understanding of intentionality, on the other hand, consciousness occupies the primary place and this indicates that there is actually one more possible form of interiorization which should be placed under the heading of intentionality. This type of interiorization consists in the insistence on will and consciousness combining in making the performer conscious of the ritual action undertaken, or that he focuses on the prescribed meaning of the act. The opposite of this is a mechanical performance accompanied by daydreaming or the habitual wandering of thoughts (i.e. a mere virtual intention). This type of interiorization thus tries to bring about a reflexive consciousness engaging the will in a second order activity. The person is then occupied with the concrete ritual action being performed, but simultaneously tries to keep in mind that he or she is performing precisely these ritual acts, and in this effort at concentration perhaps also trying to focus on their prescribed meanings. But, when ritual performance is demanding, it is probable that the sum total of will power and mental attention is absorbed into the effort of acting in a correct manner, erasing the reflexive consciousness. We could call this form of interiorization for an interiorization with a focus on concentration, to distinguish it from the focus on a certain purpose or motive. This concentration on either the ritual action itself or its meaning is then made into a condition for ritual efficacy—without it the ritual is considered fruitless or objectionable.

Interiorization which focuses on intentionality (often combined with a focus on moral purity and feelings) can be perceived as a threat within a ritual tradition, in fact opposing the very process of ritualization. We can see this, for example, in a Jewish context, in the opposition toward a Hassidic focus on interiority in prayer which devalued the study of the Torah and the Halakhah when done without the right intentions. Such a focus on intentionality easily leads to non-ritual actions also becoming empowered in a similar way as rituals, erasing the line between ritual and action in general and in so doing promoting a process of deritualization:

> This radical conception of divine immanence served as the doctrinal basis for some of the ways Hasidism renewed divine worship. Prominent among these were the raising up of "alien thoughts" and worship in corporeality. The latter term means that even mundane actions, such as eating and drinking, may be regarded as worship of God if the proper intention accompanies them. (Etkes 2002: 189)

One of our earlier examples, the Islamic notion of martyrdom, has been used in a similar way:

> For Muslim legists and theologians, what mattered was not primarily the external performance of an act but the intention with which it was

performed. There was no reason, then, why the value of martyrdom couldn't be transferred to other pious acts so long as the intention was to testify to the truth. Martyrs include not only those who die in battle but also those who testify to the truth through argument; those engaged in the jihad of the pen are thus equally eligible for the privileges of martyrdom. (Brown 2002: 108–9)

The connection which appears to exist between intentionality and deritualization motivates a more extensive treatment of ritual interiorization and intentionality. This potential disruption of rituality will be dealt with more extensively in the next chapter that focuses on the relationship between ritualization and interiorization.

THE METAPHORICAL NATURE OF INTERIORITY

In many texts dealing with interiorization, the connection between interiority and mind is a basic and implicit premise, and in the discussion of ritual efficacy above this could also seem to be the case, but as the contrast of exterior-interior in the discussion of the physical-psychical is used in a metaphorical sense, there is a possibility of proceeding to a more fundamental level (cf. Millet 1978: 796; Johnson 1999: 29–30).[31] Such an approach leads us to first devote some attention to the spatial meaning of outer and inner and also to discuss the concomitant aspect of sensory access—thus deferring the notion of the inner as something mental for a moment and instead concentrate on interiority as that which is restricted by a boundary of some sort. This border restricts our access to a particular segment of space, thereby constituting an outside and an inside—the interior being the space contained and defined by the boundary, while the exterior by definition is of unlimited expanse. One exam-

31 Johnson's short reflection on the spatial basis of interiority is surprisingly the only indication of a conception of physical interiority in the edited book titled *Merleau-Ponty: Interiority and Exteriority, Psychic Life and the World*. Merleau-Ponty's importance for the embodiment discourse should have inspired at least some of the authors to probe the metaphor and not so easily slide into a discussion of the work of Merleau-Ponty in relation to the psychological theories of Freud and Lacan. For a discussion of "oriental metaphors" within a wider cognitive theory of metaphors, although "in-out" does not figure prominently among the examples, see Lakoff and Johnson 2003: 14–21.

ple of this is a house which through its outer walls delimits an inside in opposition to the world outside, a feature that can be replicated within the house by the division of space into storeys and rooms; you could, for example, be in the hall but not be allowed access to the dining room. A house can, moreover, be located within a garden with its own set of walls, which in their turn are situated within the city walls. This box in box quality is sometimes used within a temple complex in the service of heightening the intensity of the sacred; layers of walls increasingly restricting the access of the devotees until the chamber of the holy of the holiest, as in the temple of Jerusalem built by Herod.[32]

The spatial meaning of outer and inner is the basic root metaphor (source domain) of all other senses of exteriority and interiority, but it is not obliterated by them; the domains continue to exist side by side partially overlapping. An important result of this is that when dealing with examples of ritual interiorization, we cannot only focus on human subjectivity and psychology, but we have to anchor our taxonomies and analyses firmly in a consideration of ritual space and corporality (e.g. Grimes 2006: 101–13; Tweed 2006; Knott 2005).

To the spatial division between outside and inside, a cognitive or epistemological dimension is quite naturally attached, in this way providing the basis for one of the more important metaphorical uses of exterior and interior. The boundary (i.e., the walls)—by denying us access in a physical way—also restricts our possibility of seeing and hearing what is on the inside. One concrete example of this is when a meeting is held behind closed doors, as when the College of Cardinals in the Catholic Church is electing a new pope. The cardinals remain locked up ("con-clave") in the buildings sealed off for the election until a successor of the deceased pope is elected. When this has been achieved, a fire of the ballot papers (as well as some chemicals in the election of Benedict XVI) is made in a special stove located in the Sistine Chapel and in this way white smoke is produced which signals to all those outside that the election has come

32 E.g. Goldhill 2005: 61. An orchestration of sacredness that can be compared with the discussion of whether it is even allowed for a Jew today to visit the temple mount, as he then without knowing it could step on the holy of holies (Goldhill 2005: 14).

to an end. The cardinals are thus inside in the physical sense, being confined by the walls of the buildings, but they are also on the inside in an
epistemological sense (being insiders) in that they have privileged access
to the proceeding—a privilege that is guarded with great care, for example through the use of special guards, scanning of bugging devices, and
the covering of the windows.

Not all boundaries dividing an interior from an exterior are, however,
opaque; as in the cases of a magic circle or a house with glass walls or a
museum exhibition case. In the first example, as in all rituals, a special
world is constructed—the drawing of the magic circle temporarily creates a different and set-apart reality. We can, for example, see this in the
neo-pagan prescription of a "Pagan Ritual for General Use." The ritual
circle is initially traced around the participants and has to be dissolved
before the ceremony is ended:

> A circle should be marked on the floor, surrounding those who will
> participate in the ceremony. An altar is to be set at the center of the cir-
> cle. At the center of the altar shall be placed an image of the Goddess,
> and an incense burner placed in front of it. .... The priest now takes
> the wand, and starting at the north, draws it along the entire circle
> clockwise back to the north point, saying: The circle is sealed, and all
> herein, Are totally and completely apart, From the outside world, That
> we may glorify the Lady whom we adore. ... The priestess will then
> take the wand and tap each candle to put it out, starting at the north
> and going clockwise about the circle, while saying: Our rite draws to
> its end. O lovely and gracious Goddess, Be with each of us as we depart.
> The circle is broken! (Adler 1986: 470–72)

A ritual of the kind presented above often takes place in an enclosed
place, as in a building, although this is not a prerequisite, and in those
cases the power of holiness or taboo has to uphold the special set-apart
character of ritual space, and, in so doing, create a spiritual glass wall
(Harrington 2006: 104). This has the same function as its physical counterpart, namely to constitute the physical exteriority of the outsider,

while at the same time not removing the possibility of him or her to be interior in an epistemological sense.

The examples discussed so far have illustrated that the sense of epistemological interiority is not coextensive with spatial interiority, and that the analogy connecting these two interiorities focuses on one consequence of enclosing a space with the help of physical boundaries. This partial discrepancy between the spatial and the epistemological sense of interiority is of great importance for our discussion of ritual interiorization.

One further step in the metaphorical process moving away from the spatial meaning is when the epistemological sense is increasingly detached from the physical, and we arrive at a notion of interiority which only, or at least predominately, signifies an inside in the sense of privileged sensory or mental access. One example of this is the notions of esoteric and exoteric as applied to the writings of Aristotle. The former category is constituted by the works written for a limited circle of scholars and the latter category by those works which were designed for a less advanced auditorium. In this context, esoteric designates a competence to decode certain texts, but carries with it also the sense of belonging to a group of people more or less assembled around the creator of these texts, or, in other cases, a disseminator of teachings. Esoteric designates thus not merely something difficult to understand, but that which is revealed only to a few, to those who belong to the "inner circle."[33] As the inner space delimited by walls, this inner group is finite in distinction to the infinite number of outsiders. One can see these two meanings of "esoteric" in the definition of the *Oxford English Dictionary*:

> Of philosophical doctrines, treatises, modes of speech, etc.: Designed for, or appropriate to, an inner circle of advanced or privileged disciples; communicated to, or intelligible by, the initiated exclusively.

---

33 Cf. The notion of insider trading, of which regulation is notoriously difficult, and not always criminalized (e.g. Carlton and Fischel 1983).

Hence of disciples: Belonging to the inner circle, admitted to the esoteric teaching. (*Oxford English Dictionary* 2005)

In this context, initiation can become important, which entails that the
epistemological dimension, that is, access to knowledge, is embodied
and enacted in terms of physical boundaries, which gives tremendous
importance to the notion of door or gate as the ambivalent (liminal) link
between inside and outside. The question is not so much of a *rite de passage* effectuating the transition from one social position to another, but of
rites functioning as links between different degrees of access to knowledge, which, of course, in many cases are connected to social positions
and status. The gate becomes, then, not an efficacious sign (sacrament)
for the entrance into another type of reality, but a symbol of the neophyte
gaining access to the "esoteric" circle; he or she is thus inner in a cognitive sense, a status which, however, could be considered as accompanied
by, for example, a transformation or illumination of consciousness.[34]

The cognitive interiority of esoteric societies opens up for a consideration of the interiority of social systems in general, a feature which
has been highlighted by Niklas Luhmann (1927–1998) in his grand but
sometimes abstruse sociological theoretical oeuvre. According to him,
a social system upholds its systematic character by establishing boundaries that define what belongs to the system and what is to be reckoned as
part of the environment.[35] The input into the system is filtered (simpli-
fied), interpreted, and used according to principles of communication
established within the system (Luhmann 1982: 70–71).[36] An esoteric
society, for example, establishes an "interiority" in two ways, both which
are based on the root metaphor of spatial interiority. Firstly, as the space
delimited by the walls of a house, the interior of the system is demar-
cated and finite in distinction to the environment which is potentially
infinite. Secondly, the esoteric system differentiates between insiders
who have access to knowledge and information, and outsiders who do

---

34 For a discussion within the study of Western esotericism, see Bogdan 2007: 37–52.
35 Cf. the notion of framing in a ritual context (Handelman 2006).
36 For a criticism of Luhmann's theory from a critical realist position see Elder-Vass 2007.

not. This basic principle of secret societies is also operative, though in a lesser degree, within more open religious systems.[37] Such an interiority is analogical to the epistemological deprivation caused by the opaque nature of solid walls, and to stretch the metaphor somewhat, we could consider the extent of windows culminating in transparent walls as analogical to the degree of openness or closeness of a system: Pope John XXIII, for example, in order to illustrate what the second Vatican council was all about went to a window and opened it; the force of this metaphoric gesture was not the same as if he had opened a door (letting outsiders become insiders or vice versa), but through the opening of a window he referred symbolically to the two-way type of communication he had in mind: furnishing the outside world, that is, the environment, with a fuller knowledge of the Catholic Church and at the same time making possible a clearer view of the world from the inside.

We have so far traced the metaphorical base of epistemological interiority to the spatial meaning of being interior. If we now move our focus to the human and for a little while longer suspend the equation of inner with mental, then the interiority of the human body appears quite naturally as being of a physical nature. This division between a bodily exterior and interior is at the same time spatial and epistemological, that is, I can see your face but ordinarily not your heart. There are, nevertheless, signs of the heart working, such as the pulse and "rosy cheeks," but unless I am a heart surgeon I am not likely to see many hearts during my lifetime.

One important feature of the physical inside is that it is interior only in a relative sense, something which the heart surgeon or the pathologist autopsist experiences when taking the heart out of the body. Moreover, in a medical context, the question of what is, at a given moment, on the

---

37 This is subverted in for example the hidden activities of state espionage using secret agents who are inside a particular social system and at the same time are members of another system from which the agents receive orders and to which they give information. The status of insider/outsider becomes even more complex in the case of double agents, and in the case of infiltration of religious groups the religious dimension is added to the notion of insider status. And, vice versa, we also encounter the fear that the state is infiltrated by hostile religious groups (cf. Sperry 2005 on Muslim infiltration of the American state). In these cases, the topic is primarily access to information, but also the power of decision making.

outside and what is on the inside of the living body is interestingly not always perfectly clear:

Barriers on the Outside and the Inside

As strange as it may seem, defining what is outside and what is inside the body is not always easy, because the body has many surfaces. The skin, which is actually an organ system, is obviously outside the body. It forms a barrier that prevents many harmful substances from entering the body. Although covered by a thin layer of skin, the ear canal is usually thought of as inside the body, because it penetrates deep into the head. The digestive system is a long tube that begins at the mouth, winds through the body, and exits at the anus. Is food as it passes through this tube inside or outside of the body? Nutrients and fluid are not really inside the body until they are absorbed into the bloodstream. (Beers 2006)[38]

The quotation above deals foremost with the demarcation between the outside and the inside of the body in a spatial sense, and it is important to emphasize that this is not coextensive with the epistemological interiority of the body, both, however, being relative and not absolute.[39] The individual has in everyday life some privileged access to his bodily interior,

38 As the quotation suggests, it is the "doors" and "windows" of the body which create problems for a clear-cut division between a bodily interior and exterior. In a religious context, this ambiguity has received great attention in the formulation of rules of purity—that which leaves the body (urine, faeces, blood, etc.) and that which enters (e.g. food) is potentially radically impure (Preston 1987: 92). This phenomenon could be interpreted along the lines of an urge to uphold the individual as a unit, with body pollution, therefore, being connected both to classification (cf. Douglas 1966) and personal (bodily) identity.

39 Perhaps, it is more fitting in a medical context to consider the outside and the inside of the body as constituted by the body as a system; the in and out flows are regulated by the body-system into material for its constant replication (autopoiesis) or into waste products and harmful substances (see e.g. Luhmann's discussion of psychic systems (1995: 255–77). Inner in this sense is that which becomes part of the system. The immune system in its constant battle with bacteria and viruses, which try to become part of the system or perhaps more correctly to use it for their own replication, illustrates this nicely. For an argumentation pointing to the metaphoric relation between the representation of the immune system and the emergence of the postmodern late capitalist body, see Martin 1992.

for example through pain, but this information is vastly inferior to the knowledge made available by modern medical technology. Furthermore, also the individual has to interpret the signs of the body and—strange as it may sound—is thus to a large extent exterior in relation to his or her own body, which when subjected to such a probing for information turns into an object, an attitude which is distinctively dissimilar to the ordinary experience of the body as part of the acting subject.

We can, for example, contrast the experience I have of my teeth chewing (when not particularly focusing on this activity) with my teeth as the object of the detailed work of a dentist; the teeth then in a way stop being mine, and instead become the special domain of the dentist who claims them and acts as their guardian, and when one of them is removed this becomes even more acute (cf. McGuire 1990: 285). The knowledge (awareness) that we have of our body is thus normally as being in action; this embodied consciousness is, however, disembodied when the body becomes an object, as exemplified above, but also when the harmony between will and movement in act is disjointed, as when the body is not capable of conforming to the will, and hence emerges as a principle of inertia, an object; it makes its "dys-appearance" as argued by Drew Leder (1990: 83–84; cf. Schilling 2004: 57–65).

Furthermore, in a postmodern context, when the body is conceptualized as not having an inherent nature and therefore treated as a material for achieving some arbitrary form of perfection, it becomes an object in the sense of being a project, as evidenced in the increasing interest in cosmetic surgery, diet, cosmetics, piercing, tattoo, and the ultimate makeover, the change of one's sex (Brush 1998; Kraft 2005).

If we now turn our attention to how physical interiority is handled within ritual traditions, then we see that it by its concealed (inner) nature constitutes an ideal opportunity for the construction of an "inner" body. This is, for example, the case in some tantric yogic traditions, in which the ritual practitioner places deities within the body by touching various parts of the body—a practice which Eliade explicitly called interiorization (Eliade 1973: 211). To such visualizations and meditation techniques is often attached the notion of a subtle body, which is precisely an inner body in the sense that is not visible, while at the same time being not alto-gether spiritual in a transcendent sense. On the one hand, such a body can become a miniature copy of the world with all its cosmic levels as the underworld, the earth, and the heavens, in which among others the interiorized gods dwell. The subtle body then becomes a microcosm and can be connected to the macrocosm with the help of correspondences, in this way building up a web of efficacious relations ripe for manipulation of the macro through the micro (e.g. ritual magic) or the influence of the macro on the micro (e.g. astrology).[40]

On the other hand, the subtle body can be focused on aspects of life, power, and liberation. In that case, breathing fulfills an important part, as the circulation of air is clearly necessary for life, without which the human body dies and decomposes.[41] Upon the physical fact of breathing, however, is grafted the notion of life-energy flowing through the subtle body, or some other conception of inner body. In Vedic ritual specula-tion, for example, breath was not confined to inhalation and exhalation but covered the whole field of bodily and mental activities, all considered as breaths, that is, principles of life (Cavallin 2003). In the yogic context, the subtle body is conceptualized as made up by channels and centers (cakras) through which breath circulates. The aim is to purify the chan-nels and enable the energy (kuṇḍalinī) to rise from the lower to the higher cakras. As in the case of placing gods within the body, this is an example of ritually manipulating the inner body.

In a Daoist context, we also meet the notion of a subtle or inner body connected to the cosmos, and animated by the flowing of breath or energy (qi):

[T]he inner body is seen to be related to the external world both spa-tially and temporally. That is, the head with its powers of mind is related to the heavens, the heart to the earth, and the belly to the water

---

40 For an example (Vedic) of how complex such systems of correspondences can become, see Smith 1998 and Cavallin 2002. Cf. with the modern practice of Hindu Nāḍī astrology (Gansten 2003).

41 This fact is used in some yogic contexts as a departure for techniques of liberation, the time interval between inhalation and exhalation being methodically prolonged.

or the fiery underworld. The head houses the intellect, the power to form images and concepts, judge, and regulate ch'i (the flow and concentration of breath). Thus one of the main points of focus during meditation is the mind and its regulation. (Saso 1997: 231)

When the advancements of medical science exorcise such concepts of mystical anatomy from the interiority of the physical body, to which they were traditionally connected, the subtle body becomes instead a parallel body, more like a soul than an inside. We can compare this with the progress of exploration and the consequent mapping of the globe by assiduous cartographers. The mystical geography of, for example, the garden of Eden, the earthly paradise, cannot therefore anymore be portrayed as inhabiting a remote place on the surface of the earth (Delumeau 1995), but if believed to reside in the physical universe must either be located inside the globe or be imagined as a parallel world, another planet untouched by the sins of humankind—a theme, for example, partially explored in C. S. Lewis's space trilogy. We can compare this with Thomas Aquinas's answer to the topographical argument against a corporeal paradise:

Objection 3. Further, although men have explored the entire habitable world, yet none have made mention of the place of paradise. Therefore apparently it is not a corporeal place.

Reply to Objection 3. The situation of paradise is shut off from the habitable world by mountains, or seas, or some torrid region, which cannot be crossed; and so people who have written about topography make no mention of it. (Aquinas 1947, Part 1, Q. 102, Art. 1)

However, parallel with the minute exploration of the human body by medical science, we have in the late twentieth century witnessed the advent of alternative medicine and the New Age movement on a global scale; the inner body with its energies has thus returned with a vengeance, but in a pseudoscientific outfit on the global market, exploring and exploiting the connection between physical and psychic interiority (e.g. Hanegraaff 1998: 42–61; Löwendahl 2002).

The various notions of a subtle (inner) body is a reminder that we have to be cautious in using the Western medical body as an instrument of explanation when analyzing religious traditions: the interior of the physical body is inner not only in the sense of being contained by the surface, but is also inner in the sense of being partially hidden, even to the subject itself, and this makes the physical interior fertile ground for the religious imagination. It enables the religious traditions to introject the whole cosmos into the body, at the same time as this interior landscape is modeled on (or linked to) bodily phenomena such as breathing, eating, warmth and coldness, expulsion of substances, etc., in short, on the living human body, and its capacities for, if not immortality, then at least health and long life. The interior of the physical body can thus become both the landscape of salvation and a ritual arena, a space plastic to the mind and the cultural forces, while at the same time vital in the literal sense of the word.

INTERIORIZATION OF RITUAL PERFORMANCE

The dual nature of the human interior (physical and mental) provides us with a basis for the subdivision of interiorized ritual performances, as a ritual can be enacted on an inner physical arena or within the mind using the creativity of imagination. In the latter case, that is, when the entire ritual is performed in the mind only, mental attitude does not have to be given special significance—the movements and utterances, that is, the exterior aspects of ritual, are merely imagined in the same manner as they would have been exteriorly performed. A parallel case within the modern world of sports is when a professional skier goes through the race mentally before the actual performance. The skier, or the ritual practitioner, thus visualizes the movements before his inner eye, the imagination. The skier could do this as a preparation for the enactments of the movements, but he could also add a special mental attitude, for example, some form of positive thinking. These two, that is, mental attitude and mental carrying out, need, however, not be combined. There exists within Hinduism already in the Vedic period, for example, the option of performing a ritual solely with the mind, manasā.[42] And in later tantric traditions, visualization of deities within the body of the worshipper occupies an important place:

> The Jayākhya describes a process of visualisation for establishing the supreme Lord within the heart as envisaged as a throne (antaramānasa-yāga). During the inner worship, the practitioner visualises the hierarchical cosmos in the forms of deities located within his own body. (Flood 2006: 116)

This inner ritual, however, was combined with outer rituals and was, therefore, not part of a radical deritualization, but merely extended the ritual scene to the inner body[43]—something which then can be seen as ritualization actually expanding, covering even more aspects of the person, with other words, the direct opposite of deritualization.

There is also, as mentioned above, one type of interiorized ritual performance that does not focus on the mind, but on physical interiority. These rituals are physically performed within the human body, in this way situating the normally exterior aspects of ritual action within the body. The problem is that it is not easy to isolate this form of interiorization from an engagement with a mentally inner body, as the tantric body referred to above. The pressing question is where the physical interiority ends and the mental takes over. The difficulties associated with trying to provide an answer to this question is due to the fact that the physically inner being is hard to ritualize as it is largely beyond the control of the human will. We therefore get a sliding scale between physical interiorization and mental performance, for example in the conception of

---

42 For an example of a mental (manasā "by the mind") ritual performance, see Śatapatha brāhmaṇa 10. 5. 3. 1–3 (Eggeling 1966 [1882]).

43 Vedic sacrifices are still performed, for example the 1975 Agnicayana performance in India was filmed and commented upon by a team of scholars headed by Frits Staal, the outcome being a massive two-volume work (Staal 1983) and a rather short film compared with the extensive footage. For criticism on the project, focusing on anachronism and lack of reflexivity, see Schechner 1987.

a subtle (inner) body in which streams of energy flow in special vessels; an energy that can be ritually manipulated both through purely mental operations as visualizations and through more physical processes. The mentally constructed body is in this way grafted on the physical body which provides it with sensations such as warmth, density, pain, tension, and excitement.

If we try to focus on the more physical pole of the scale of this inner body then ritualization could either be effectuated through manipulating those processes which are (at least partially) under the control of the will, such as breathing or eating, or the surface could be perforated as in the case of acupuncture, or melted down as in the act of laying of hands with the intention of effectuating an inner healing or an inner spiritual transformation. Laying on of hands could alternatively be viewed more as a sign of a spiritual and thus a non-spatial influence between two persons, than an actual physical process as the transferral of some kind of energy. Physically interior performance is thus either dependent upon gaining control over the inner physical body by willpower, or has to rely upon the penetration or effacement of the surface (and thus also the interior–exterior divide). Within hatha yoga this ritual conquest of the interiority of the body is carried to extreme lengths as, for example, in the exercise of swallowing a long cloth and then retrieving it, or through inflating the urethra by mechanical means with air, which enable the yogin to use it for suction instead of expulsion (e.g. Akers 2002).

A parallel process is that in many sacrifices much attention is directed to the interior of the victim, which is used as oblation; the sacrificial slaughter can in these cases be viewed as an example of ritual interiorization, the manipulation of the physically interior, with, however, the inevitable consequence that inner becomes outer—the animal turned inside out. This is given another twist in extispicy, that is: "the examination of the organs of a sacrificed animal for purposes of divination" (Pardee 2003: 291), with the inner of the animal treated as a text to be read. The ritual takes place in the interior by, for example, the examination of the liver, but the liver is no longer inner, as the spatial interiority is abolished by the uncovering of the cognitive inner. If we, however, could equip an ancient Ugarit priest with modern technology, divination with the help of the liver would be achieved without destroying the body, and the liver could also be manipulated, in a magico-religious analogue to medical diagnostics and treatment.

Another example of rituals which play on the barrier between physically interior and exterior is psychic surgery: healing rituals in which the ritual specialist seemingly extracts with his or her own hands tissue from within the body of patient, and when the blood is wiped away no trace of the operation, as a scar, is to be found on the skin. Though this would qualify as fraudulent in a medical context, what is interesting for our purposes is the construction of a physically inner ritual, on the exterior of the body, through the illusory suspension of the barrier between physically interior and exterior (Singer 1990).

INTERIORIZATION OF RITUAL EFFECTS

To a large extent, the different types of interiorization of the effects produced by ritual means parallel those of ritual efficacy. In the same manner as efficacy can be considered dependent on moral purity, feelings, knowledge, spiritual qualities, and intentionality, there are ritual effects such as feelings, virtues, or gnosis. It can, however, be argued that to consider the effect of a ritual to be the creation of a certain kind of intentionality will not form a basis for the construction of a relevant category of interiorization, at least not in the meaning of purpose, that is, the intended effect. To then say that the effect of the ritual would be to dispose the performer to intend certain effects carries with it an intrinsic indeterminateness, for also these intended effects have to be specified if we are to get a clearer view of this type of interiorization. If one then defines the effect as outside of the person, e.g. healthy cattle, then one has partially escaped the interior through the directed character of intentionality. In order to have a prime example of interiorization, an interior intended effect also has to be specified, as gnosis. The argument could appear as overly subtle, but the point is that if the ritual is believed to produce an altered state of intentionality, this entails that such an effect is interior in being intentional, but could be exterior in the effect or object intended by the one whose intentionality has been altered. This type of interiorization thus focuses either on it being an intentional state that is produced, or on what the produced intention is directed to, as in the example above: knowledge; but the list is open (feelings, physical objects, etc.). The question is thus in what sense such an interiorization differs from the stipulation of the effect of the ritual as precisely gnosis. The simple answer is that the distinction is between, on the one hand, the actual producing of gnosis through a ritual and, on the other hand, the awakening of the will in a person to achieve such gnosis.

We can also adduce as more evidence for the relevance of this distinction further types of rituals aimed at changing the will of another person. The effect of such a ritual is neither gnosis, nor a feeling or a virtue, but a will to do something specific. In love spells, a feeling or desire is, however, often linked to the effected new inclination of the will. We can witness this connection in the following narrative from the vita of Saint Hilarion, in which he exorcises a demon from a virgin—the possession having been caused by a love spell inscribed by a young man on a curse tablet and buried under her threshold:

> In that same town of Gaza a young man fell desperately in love with a virgin of God who lived nearby. He repeatedly touched her, joked with her, nodded at her, whispered to her, and did other things like this, the sort of things that tend to herald the destruction of virginity. But he got nowhere. So he journeyed to Memphis, so that, after disclosing his wound, he might return armed with magical techniques to use against the virgin. Accordingly, after a year of instruction by the priests of Asclepius, who do not cure souls but ruin them, he came back bursting for the fornication he had anticipated in his mind. He inscribed some verbal monstrosities and monstrous forms on plates of Cyprian bronze and buried them under the threshold of the girl's house. At once the virgin went mad. She cast off her veil, she swung her hair around, she gnashed her teeth, she shouted out the young man's name. The enormity of her love had transformed itself into frenzy. So

her parents brought her to the monastery and handed her over to the old man. At once the demon howled and confessed, "I was the victim of force and kidnapped against my will. How well I used to deceive men with dreams in Memphis! O the tortures and torments I suffer! You compel me to come out, but I am held in bonds under the threshold. I cannot come out unless the young man that holds me dismisses me." (Ogden 2002: 230)

One should note that in this example the altered will of the girl is accomplished by the intrusion of another intentional agent. If this possession was effected contrary to the intentions of the girl, then this amounts to the use of spiritual force, and leaves her will more suspended than changed; that is, if we stick to the presentation in the narrative. Within a psychological analytical framework, the same condition could be interpreted as the conflict between different intra-psychological forces, the demon being a personification of desire. The point of interiorization is, however, that a ritual act is believed to have inner effects, whether that corresponds to actual facts is another matter.

Another form of interior effects is that pertaining to the inner physical body. As physical interiority is a relative notion depending on sensory and cognitive access, and as effects in the body naturally manifest themselves both in the hidden interior and in the manifest exterior, we get a somewhat fluid category. A natural candidate for this category is constituted by rituals designed to strengthen the interior vital powers, and those intended to heal interior physical dysfunctions. The question is, nevertheless, when we should deem healings as foremost interior and when as predominately exterior, for the cure of an interior ailment often also removes exterior symptoms, and, as a result, affects the whole person. Normally the cure of a psychological defect or a psychosomatic complex with a psychological cause would primarily qualify as interior healings, but with our emphasis on the interior as both mental *and* physical also the disappearance of a tumor in the abdomen would qualify as an interior effect. This is important as healing frequently includes not only a separate physically interior healing and a connected restored psychological equilibrium, but the interior in a religious context is often an inner body not identical with the model generated by Western medical science.

Inner healing can thus be considered as potentially taking place on three different levels, which correspond to three kinds of effects. In the first place, a healing ritual could be seen as having an interior psychological effect, as when the Roman empress Faustina, who had fallen in love with a gladiator, was advised to bath in his blood in order to be cured (Ogden 2002: 229); the effect in this case was both of intention and feelings. Or the healing could be of a spiritual nature, as the cancellation of original sin in the Christian baptism, or the decrease of the karmic residue in a Hindu context. Or finally, the healing could be primarily of a physical nature as in the following narrative:

> It was at this moment M. Perrin felt a strange warmth in his toes which up to then had felt numb and almost dead. Next he realised his feet were coming back to life, and warmth beginning to spread through his body. ... Attributing this to cardiac insufficiency, he thought it was the end! However, the heat spread through his legs, and he stirred in his wheelchair. (Glynn 2003: 89)

DIVINE INTERIORITY

Up to this point, the focus has mainly been on human interiority, but in most religious rituals this epistemologically restricted area has, as previously alluded to, a counterpart, namely, the realm of the supernatural: comprising gods, demons, ghosts, and ancestors. In the same manner as human interiority, the gods are not accessible through normal perception, though religious narrative and poetry abound with examples of close encounters with superhuman agents. Interiorization as the anchoring of different aspects of ritual action and discourse in the hidden realms of human interiority is then paralleled with the similar tendency of locating, for example, ritual efficacy in the divine sphere. The ritual is then not ultimately grounded in the correct observance of the ritual norms, nor in any special condition of human physical or mental interiority, but rests on, for example, the decisions of divine will. In that case, the foundation of ritual power is interior in the sense of being hidden, but not with necessity located within any of the human ritual participants. The efficacy becomes dependent on the exterior aspects of the ritual only as a means to influence the divine will. But, as with all interiorities, also this has to be externalized; the divine will must, therefore, be materialized (manifested) in some concrete sign, that is, if it is to be known. It could be achieved by mechanical divination processes, as the ancient Chinese (Shang dynasty) method of cracking, with the help of a heated object (a red-hot stick), flat bones (e.g. shoulder blades of cattle) which previously had been inscribed with signs. The cracks were interpreted as signs of the will of the gods, as direct answers to the questions posed (Adler 2002: 22). Or the divine will can be expressed through a human medium temporarily possessed by the spirit in question. It is easy to see that such sign production—when it becomes ritualized—could succumb to processes moving away from the hidden, interior aspects; the sign itself becomes the guarantor of ritual efficacy.

In one sense, the divine ritual participant or addressee is on the same level as the human participants; an agent among agents, but with the decisive difference that the divine agent is totally interior in the sense of being hidden. The focus therefore cannot be on divine exteriority in the meaning of behavior, as it is invisible, but has to be manifested by signs or enacted by human actors who could be deemed to be possessed by the God, or acting in its place, for example in persona Christi. The various divine or infernal interiorities open up the possibility that while no part of human interiority is considered important for ritual efficacy, the hidden spiritual world could be believed to be crucial.

We can take the consideration of the divine part of human ritual one step further through the observation that divine will is not only of decisive importance for ritual felicity—gods are very often treated as ritually active in their own right. Such ritual activity is eminently interior and can be externalized in various ways. One type is when the human ritual is considered as parallel with a similar though much more perfect heavenly ritual, which functions as its paradigm, the source of its power and legitimacy—with the human ritual being then the enactment of this lofty prototype. Such heavenly rituals can besides strengthening ritual activity reveal itself to a select human being, the clouds of heaven temporarily drawing apart to reveal the heavenly liturgy in all its splendor. If the visionary is transported in spirit to that realm, his or her participation in the Divine Liturgy is possible, though probably requiring taxing purifications. In a similar way, more sinister magical practices could be grounded in the belief that they are reflections of infernal liturgies from which they draw their energy.

The gods are also very often treated as participants in the human rituals, invited as guests and treated with honor. As it is difficult to interact with invisible agents, they have to be represented (externalized) in some way within the exterior machinations of the ritual proceedings. In an elaborate Hindu *pūjā*, for example, the god is represented by a statue (in a personal or non-personal form) which is awoken, bathed, fed, and honored in various ways: the god in his or her turn distributes blessings. If such a representation of a god is subjected to processes moving away from interiority, then ritual efficacy can be seen to lie in the exterior aspects of the treatment of the statue—becoming more or less synonymous with the deity. The corresponding transformation of performance is then the tendency to consider the god-statue as acting primarily from a position within the physical realm: the god of the statue becomes in this way localized—you have to travel to the shrine in order to address it and so forth. Exteriorization of the spiritual hidden parts of rituals, therefore, entails a reification of the culturally produced images and objects: they cease to be signs and become powerful agents in their own right, despite the possible theological incorrectness of such an attitude.

Furthermore, different kinds of interiorities can become interconnected, as when, for example, the interiority of the divine is linked with human physical and psychical interiority. The gods then reside within the body as in forms of tantrism, or human interiority is postulated as the same as the transcendent divine, *tat tvam asi*: Brahman and Ātman sharing the same elusive nature. Exteriorization, in such a context, could be the insistence that both human interiority and the invisible gods are dependent for their power and well-being upon the correct performance of the ritual acts.

This exercise in extending the concept of interiority should alert us to the existence of even further areas of interiority, for example the physical interiority and exteriority created by screens or walls in a sanctuary restricting the number of people allowed to enter, as in the Jagannath temple where non-Hindus are not allowed, and the admittance of dalits is a sensitive issue. And all these interiorities (human physical and mental interiority, the interiority of the gods, the spatial interiority of the temple, etc.) can become linked and are subject to the same semiotic processes of having to be expressed by means of signs, or enacted as actually manifesting themselves: the gods walking among men. We should not here be blind to the importance of social interiority linked to power and inequality, which is so conspicuous in the case of the Jagannath temple, which provides an interesting twist as the dalits were allowed to peep through some holes in the temple walls, gaining an epistemological interiority while remaining physically, ritually, and socially exterior.

The main task of this chapter has been to indicate the many forms interiorization in a ritual context can take. To focus on the human interior is not simply to make spirituality important, but to comprise a set of different strategies that move the social and individual attention toward what is hidden and epistemologically problematic—areas that can be located within the body or within the mind (soul) or both at the same time. These processes of interiorization strive in the opposite direction of ritualization which labors to exteriorize the action under consideration to render it intersubjective. However, not all forms of interiorization challenges the pivotal point of ritualization, namely, the ritual commitment, and concrete rituals are built up by both exteriorizing and interiorizing practices. And it is to this dynamic relationship between exteriority and interiority that we now turn.

CHAPTER THREE

The Interaction of Interiorization and Ritualization

Through the two previous chapters, a profile of both interiorization and ritualization has been built up which enables us to continue with a discussion of their relationship. The point is not to reduce this relationship to a simple formula, which in fact has been made impossible by the division of interiorization into several subcategories. We should instead strive toward a representation of the rich tapestry of ritual life as a field of different interactions between *inter alia* ritualization processes and emphases on human interiority—sometimes reinforcing each other, at other times striving in opposing directions. One can continue in this spirit and elaborate on the texture of the ritual field by adding a consideration of the level of performativity; the connections with social structure and power; links with religious mythology; and aesthetical qualities and operative biological needs and constraints. It is a segment of this web of interactions that we call a ritual. Ritualization provides it with a basic character which makes the framed actions "objective," but that is certainly not all there is to a ritual. In the following pages, a modest attempt to broaden the discussion of interiorization will be made by placing ritualization within, on the one hand, the relation between exteriorization and interiorization, and, on the other hand, between externalization and internalization, both which are conceptual pairs founded on the opposition between inner and outer, manifested respectively as interior–exterior and internal–external. However, the disruptive potential inherent in such a complex nexus of relations has to be acknowledged, which makes it necessary to bring into the discussion also the opposite process of ritualization: deritualization. The ritual commitment can thus be abandoned, outright rejected, or simply fade away, leaving room for new forms of ritual practice or the logic of expanding forms of instrumental rationality.

EXTERIORIZATION – INTERIORIZATION

Exteriorization, in the same manner as externalization, signifies a movement toward what is outer or exterior, and figures in many contexts with this basic meaning, but specified to fit the domain in question (see e.g. Løgstrup 1995: 262). In 1975, Ronald Grimes wrote a short article on masks in a ritual context and used the notion in the very title: "Masking: Toward a Phenomenology of Exteriorization." However, exteriorization does not figure prominently in the article, though the divide interior–exterior does, as in the following quote: "Even though the Dogon Great Mask is not worn, it is a semblance of an exteriority which iconographically presupposes a human or divine interiority" (Grimes 1975: 509). Instead of exteriorization, or with the intention of complementing it, Grimes, therefore, introduces the notion "concretion," which carries with it the meanings above given to materialization and externalization, that is, "a bodying forth or fixing of an external power" (ibid.). As this meaning of movement from the interior to the exterior was assigned to the notion of externalization, ritual exteriorization shall in the following instead be considered as the opposite process of interiorization. As interiorization signifies the shifting of focus from the exterior to the interior, exteriorization is the process in which the focus is directed to the exterior at the expense of the interior. Frits Staal, for example, in his book *Advaita and Neoplatonism* discusses interiorization, but also the notion of exteriorization, arguing that the Vedic ritual development was from a stage in which no difference was made between inner and outer to one in which an increasing exteriorization eventually led to a reaction of interiorization. He does not go into details of what exteriorization really is, but it seems to coincide with the growing complexity of the Vedic śrauta sacrifices and the mechanistic interpretation of ritual efficacy (Staal 1961: 71–72; Bodewitz 1973: 328–29, however, objects against such an explanation).

When contrasted with interiorization, exteriorization signifies the processes that instead of assigning importance to the interior aspects of ritual—which are not revealed in an immediate way to the senses of the ritual practitioners and the scholars doing fieldwork—emphasize the exterior features of action. When comparing the notion of exteriorization with that of externalization, it is important to stress that the former does not denote the outpouring of actions and discourses from the interior of the individual onto the intersubjective arena, but signifies the strategy of emphasizing the exterior aspects of ritual acts, either in actual performance or in the regulation and interpretation of rituals.

One problem which presents itself when one defines exteriorization accordingly is that rituals seem by definition to be exterior—something which prompted Staal to conceptualize Vedic ritual change as a fall from a primordial monist condition to a dualism in which the exterior increasingly took over, initiating an interiorizing reaction. However, he later formulated a general theory of ritual which insisted on the essential separation of meaning and ritual action, thus advocating the "meaninglessness" of ritual (Staal 1989). Rituals portrayed in this way are essentially and primordially formal, with interiorizing interpretations emerging as semiotic cosmetics on the pure face of ritual form.[44] By connecting ritualization with conceptual abstraction in chapter one, we have considerably narrowed this gulf separating ritual action and meaning. What now lies before us is to put ritualization into this wider perspective of forms of exteriorization in order to delineate how these can be related to interiorizing tendencies within ritual traditions.

The interiorization of ritual efficacy was, as mentioned above, divided into several subcategories. One type, for example, singles out knowledge as the prerequisite for ritual efficacy. The corresponding form of exteriorization, then, emphasizes that the knowledge status of the performer has no (or little) consequences for ritual efficacy. Instead the gestures in themselves can be seen to guarantee the correct mechanism of

---

44 For the debate aroused by Staal's theory, see e.g. Smith 1991 and Staal's reply, 1993, and also Penner, 1985, which refers to an article of Staal written before *Rules Without Meaning*, but expressing the same ideas, and the three articles in *Religion* (21) in 1991 by Allen Grapard, Burton Mack, and Ivan Strenski, which were answered by Staal in the same volume.

the ritual, but this needs not be the case, or we can instead come across cases where another type of interiorization is in place. For example, although the knowledge of the performer is not vital, the piety could be; that is, the appropriate feelings for approaching a divine person with an offering must be in place for the ritual to be efficacious. Exteriorization, then, constitutes a negation of the efficacy of a particular interior aspect—in this case knowledge—and in order to give exteriorization a more positive content, one must specify a particular exterior aspect which is selected for its ritual efficacy—the most probable being ritual gestures and utterances, of which scrupulous and correct performance is in focus.

One complication in this endeavor to delineate interiorization and exteriorization, already alluded to, is that the very process of ritualization carries with it a tendency toward exteriorization, as the action by being ritualized is made independent of the interior life of the individual performer. Exteriorization hence appears to be the default position when an action is ritualized, or at least a closely connected process. But we can also use the concept of exteriorization in this context to signify the continuation of an impulse already inherent in ritualization, and, in this way, emphasize this tendency even further. If we stick to our first species of exteriorization, the exteriorization focusing on knowledge, one would expect that the ritualization of a meal with invited divine guests—with other words the creation of a sacrifice—would not make the knowledge status of the human participants initially overwhelmingly important: the most likely outcome is that in a first phase this is not a manifest question in ritual discourse. But interiorization with a focus on knowledge probably asserts itself rather early in a variety of ways, for example through the importance given to initiation or through the development of ritual specialists. An interiorizing position can also arise which emphasizes gnosis as the most important ingredient in ritual activity—with exteriorization, by denying gnosis its vital role, then becoming a strategy to enhance the legitimacy of an ordained priesthood, or merely a way to guarantee that ritual validity is based upon intersubjectively available factors. The point made here is that although ritualization carries with it a certain tendency toward exteriorization as the default position in regard to ritual efficacy, when we actually analyze ritual traditions, we are confronted with a complex web of interrelated tendencies and strategies of interiorization and exteriorization. One should thus be aware of the danger in trying to construct an evolutionary scheme of ritual development in the sense that in the beginning all rituals were through and through exterior before giving way to interiorizing tendencies. The actual balance between these two tendencies in all their different forms in a specific ritual tradition is an empirical fact and cannot be decided *a priori*. However, this does not prohibit us against uncovering historical developments, but rather warns us against oversimplified chronological charts. It also alerts us to the temptation of letting a redemptive monism slip into our explanations, that is, the tendency to assert either that rituals are in essence exterior (e.g. formal behavior) while interiority is accidental, or, the other way around, emphasizing the interior part of rituals (e.g. the ethical dimension), while lashing out toward the dangers of ritualism, the sterility of elite formalism, and the insufficiency of a "magical" worldview.

When dealing with purity as a condition for ritual efficacy, the consideration of interiority and exteriority becomes somewhat complicated since ablutions and purifications seem to be universal features of religious rituals. In a first step, we therefore have to consider precisely what kind of purity we are dealing with, because exteriorization in regard to ritual efficacy can manifest itself either as ritual acts considered as relying on the external material purity of the performers—that they have washed away the impurities clinging to their bodies—or as a disregard of both internal and external purity. Interiorization, on the other hand, either puts emphasis on the interior material purity or the moral, spiritual purity. This can, nevertheless, be achieved through the same means as exterior purity, for example ablutions, but also by interior means as the silent recitation of a mantra.

The dividing line between interiorization and exteriorization in regard to purity is thus dependent upon whether purity is considered as interior or as exterior. To make purity vital in a ritual context is not automatically an example of interiorization. One could in fact argue that exterior ritual purity, which comprises both physical cleanliness and the use of culturally defined "clean" materials and the avoidance of those which are considered impure, is naturally connected to the process of ritualization. Purity is an ordered condition, a construction of the individual according to specific norms and, therefore, entails a de-individualization in the same manner as ritualization. For example, the gods and their abodes are almost always considered as more pure than humans and their world. The contact or approximation with the divine (supernatural, holy, etc.) then requires some form of purification.[45] The human rising toward the divine state undergoes an act of deification, which is more or less radical depending on the intensity and status of the meeting. Purification when inducing a more pure state is, then, in a way a washing away of the individuality of the performer—a more unified condition is accomplished, in contrast to the fragmented and multifarious nature of the concrete individual, which is prone to dissolution, decomposition, and death, the most polluting state. The intersubjective immutability of objective action is reflected by tendencies toward unifying, simplifying, and abstraction, as, for example, indicated in Ronald Grimes's study of ritual masks. Purification is akin to formality and conceptual abstraction in being a method of rising above the fleeting human world to a more permanent and harmonious sphere. At the same time, it lessens the presence of individuality in order to achieve perfection or at least by temporarily approximating the ideal.

Feelings are another set of interior states which can be made points of departure for interiorization, in this way making feelings important for ritual efficacy: you have to feel in a certain way for the ritual to work. The corresponding exteriorization simply makes feelings unimportant for the consideration of ritual efficacy. However, it can manifest itself in another way due to the semiosis that interior states are wont to undergo when made into foci for intersubjective cultural processes. When crying is made into a sign of interior pain, and so long it is read as a sign and

---

45 For the prominent place of purification in Shinto ritualism, for example, see Clarke 1994: 118ff.

the signified subjective pain experience is in focus, we are dealing with a case of interiorization. But when the enactment of the sign in itself becomes the condition of efficacy, we have a case of exteriorization. The exterior aspect of crying, that is, the crying behavior, can be increasingly ritualized, disconnecting the behavior from the interior state. The crying gestures are then formalized and can be enacted by any skilled performer. Such a stylization (abstraction) could be carried to a point where the connection with the notion of pain is lost altogether and we are confronted with an example of pure formalism relying exclusively on normative rationality or drifting in the direction of aesthetical values. Such an enactment of emotional behavior can, however, have its therapeutic advantages as in the case of professional mourners or those compelled to mourn their enemies (Alexiou 1974: 10).

If we move on to spiritual qualities, exteriorization can, for example, consist in the insistence on the amount of accumulated karma being of no consequence for the efficacy of the ritual act. In the same manner as the disregard of interior purity and feelings, this type of exteriorization adds to the abstract nature of ritual performance as the actors become even more exchangeable when their spiritual constitution does not matter. On the other hand, when we encounter an interiorizing trend in this regard, that is, when the spiritual constitution is important for the ritual to work properly, then the individuality of the performers becomes important; at the same time, as argued previously, the hidden nature of the interior makes it necessary with outward signs of the spiritual qualities. And if this sign is caught up in a process of exteriorization, it becomes severed from the interior spiritual state of the performer and the sign as an object in itself becomes the criteria for ritual efficacy.

The last opposition between interiorization and exteriorization to be mentioned in regard to ritual efficacy is that between making individual intentionality important or unimportant for the ritual to be reckoned as a successful performance, and thus not a failure. As intentionality previously was divided into intention, motive, and purpose, we have to consider these principles one by one. When beginning with intention one meets the problem that accrued to the consideration of the "intention of the Church" in Catholic doctrine, namely, that the individual performer has to make an act of will to conform to the stipulated intention of the sacrament. This opens up for the consideration that although two ritual acts look completely alike they can belong to different types of actions. For example, making the sign of the cross, or scratching oneself in four places, or making the gestures as part of a curse. If a ritual tradition moves in an exteriorizing direction in this aspect then also the unconscious performing of the gestures in the right context will count as a successful performance and thus yield the expected results. The individual intention, that is, the understanding of the type of action performed, will not alter its efficacy. On the other hand, if the individual intention is seen as crucial then we get the problems which confront the evaluation of sacramental efficacy in a Catholic context, namely, that this deviant intention must somehow be externalized, in order to be evaluated. The default position is then, if not otherwise indicated, that the individual intention is considered in line with the socially stipulated intention.

Exteriorization in regard to individual motive and purpose makes the goal of the performer of no importance for the validity and success of the ritual. Performing the ritual with the object of achieving holiness or great fame is, therefore, not a factor indicating whether the ritual works or not. Such a type of exteriorization can go hand in hand with an increasing ritualization as a reaction to interiorizing tendencies. The rituals are then extended over more and more space and time of the lifeworld of the individual, coupled with the notion that it is the scrupulous executing of all the ritual details that are essential for the efficacy. Or, even the notion of efficacy can be lost so that the rituals become their own goals. But eventually such a high degree of ritualization must be founded either on divine command, ethnic identity, or similar principles as it is very costly and impractical (limiting the zones for instrumental rationality).

The exteriorization of ritual performance signifies the process of letting all ritual proceedings take place in the intersubjective arena, shunning the hidden realm of the interior. Also this type of exteriorization seems to go hand in hand with ritualization, and a conscious strategy emphasizing the intersubjective aspect of performance is then probably in most cases a reaction to a previous process of placing the ritual acts in the interior. That is, for the most part, when a ritual is created it concerns exterior performance: intersubjectively accessible actions. Exteriorization cannot in this phase take place other than as the prohibition of interior performance, due to the fact that what is externalized is already exterior. It is as a secondary process of making what was interior exterior that exteriorization comes into sight as an independent course of action.

The third aspect of rituals that was considered as prone to interiorizing was the effects of the ritual. For even if the ritual is performed in the exterior and believed to be totally dependent for its efficacy on the exterior actions, then the effects could still be mentally interior as illumination, feelings, virtues, interior purity, or physically interior—as the healing of an interior organ. When also the effects are exteriorized then we instead come across effects as the multiplication of cattle, success in war, or peace. One interesting feature of the exteriorization of ritual effects is that this process does not go hand in hand with ritualization in the same way as exteriorization of efficacy and performance. This is due to the fact that the effect of the ritual is mostly not in itself ritualized, but is merely the extra-ritual fruit of the ritual acts.

All these different types of exteriorization minimize the importance of inner life of the individual performer of little for the evaluation of when a ritual act is to be reckoned as a successful performance or a failure. In extreme cases, the efficacy, thereby, becomes solely dependent upon exterior performance—the accurate enactment of the ritual norms; and ritual action wholly takes place on "the outside," where its fruits also manifest themselves. Exteriorization and ritualization seem to go hand in hand and their mutual amplification adds to the impersonal and formal atmosphere of rituals, and could—when especially powerful—result in a standpoint that while extending the scope of ritual injunction accords little attention toward the hidden, private aspects of individuals and hence have special problems (and attractions) within a culture that celebrates interiority and individuality.

INTERNALIZATION

If ritualization is foremost a process of abstraction which entails a de-individuation of the person, then a focus within a ritual tradition on the human interior seems to go in the opposite direction. As the interior is equivalent to the hidden features of the person, the intersubjective dimension of ritual activity is subjected to a gravitational pull toward the subjective. However, it is not only the interior of the human person which is hidden, but also the ideal world shares this elusive nature, despite its being maintained within the social group through such public means as discourse, rituals, and institutions. The ideal entities having shed matter through the process of abstraction are not in a direct sense part of the empirical world, although many states of affairs are interpreted as instances of their manifestation or personification, as the oracle in Delphi or a crying Madonna. As argued previously, signs and sign systems such as symbols and natural languages mediate between the ideals and actual social life, between the human interior and the expectations of the social group. Ritualization enables the individual and the group to ascend and benefit from the abstract realm, but in order to create and maintain a self which is in harmony with the social identity offered to the individual, also the interior of the person has to be reached. In this process, ritualization itself is not enough, as it strives in the opposite direction, laboring to de-individuate the person. Ritualization, in a sense, suspends the subjective in order to allow the person to benefit from the power of the ideal entities.

One could expect that the solemnity of rituals achieves the transformation of the human interior without much ado, but at the heart of the matter there is a tension between, on the one hand, this transformation into a sign and molded according to a semiotic logic, and, on the other hand, not confining the transformation merely to the level of persona, but letting it reach the self, both in its aspect of personal identity and the aspects of the self which fall outside of it. This is in a nutshell the process of internalization. Through it, the ideal entities of the cultural and religious world are made part of the self, or, with other words, they transform the self in accordance with their nature. It is, therefore, necessary that this anchoring of the exterior in the interior is part of the ritual itself, though it stands in a tense relation to the abstract nature of the ritual persona. If internalization fails on a large scale, then a ritual tradition faces serious problems in maintaining its existence, or develops into a cold formalism in which the preservation of the rituals and their development have to rely entirely on the force of the ritual injunction.

How is this influencing of the self achieved? One way is to activate feelings within the ritual through different means, such as nocturnal gatherings with burning torches, muttered prayers, rhythmic beating of drums, the affliction of pain to the neophyte, fasting, vigils, the climactic slaughter of an animal, experiences of pleasure and beauty in the form of sounds, colors, and fragrances, sublime architecture, the shame of public confession and so on (Glucklich 2001). These are processes which effectively work below the level of reason and discourse, and influence us directly as bodily creatures. When this functions, the ideal is internalized—situated within the person—but is also in a special way connected to the person as embodied: feelings being eminently mental and bodily at the same time. Emotional activation is, however, not a subspecies of interiorization though it affects the interior, because it does not connect the efficacy, goal, or performance of the ritual to the interior. For example, a nocturnal vigil and fast before an important ritual most probably activate a series of feelings, but to say that the efficacy of the ritual hinges on whether these feelings are felt is another matter. The use of emotions is very helpful in achieving the goal of making the ideal internal to the person, or at least to create some attachment to it. That is to say, although the ideal (the particular notion, narrative, or god) is not completely understood by the individual, he or she nevertheless feels that the ideal as it is represented is important, embodies positive values, is desirable, and the ideal could in that form become part of the individual's self—conceptually diffuse but emotionally important.

The internalization of the ideal, including ritual norms, can also be achieved on the level of signs, that is, through discourse and symbols. One way of doing this is naturally through teaching and instruction. The student is made to memorize elements of cosmology, eschatology, and ethics either in the form of narrative or in a more abstract form made easier to remember through mnemonic techniques as lists or formulas. When it comes to ritual norms, however, the most efficient method is learning by doing, conditioning the body to behave in a certain way. In the same manner as emotional activation, this process of learning can start much earlier than the intellectual maturity necessary for discursive instruction allows. Through acts as kneeling, silence, or dancing, the body of the child is ritualized; the ritual norms are made into natural ways of acting, they become integral parts of the person, partly subconscious, and when combined with emotional activation, the internalization of the ritual is achieved almost without requiring any discursive level at all.

However, when we instead follow the special action logic of ritual acts, internalization comes close to the meaning of interiorization—internalization being then the ritual act of making the ideal internal to the person. Through discourse this is achieved by understanding, while in a ritual this is realized by, for example, concretely inhaling or swallowing the ideal, be it a person, force, or virtue. What is eaten enters into the interior, nourishes it, and becomes part of the person, or what is eaten is evil and poisonous and makes the person sick. A ritual meal is, therefore, on the conceptual level an eating of ideals, as we have to see the act of eating as abstracted from matter. The ideal entity is mostly located on the intermediate level of abstraction, that is, it is personified; for example, the Christian Eucharist is the eating of Christ and only secondary of the abstract godhead. But it could also be concepts which are eaten as strength, love, or purity. Taking this one step further, not merely the symbol is digested and with it its meaning, but discourse itself could enter into the metabolic process of making meaning interior. But how is one to eat discourse? The simplest way is to eat it in its textual form. In the Bible we find several examples of this. The first is an ordeal, described in Numeri (the fourth book of Moses) 5: 12–29, prescribing the following procedure for a husband suspecting that his wife has been unfaithful. He takes her to the priest, bringing with him materials for a small offering (an offering of jealousy). The priest then pours holy water into

an earthen vessel and mixes some dust into the liquid. The woman holding the cereal offering in her hands listens while the priest pronounces
a curse with the meaning that if she is innocent then the bitter water
will do her no harm, but if guilty it will make her stomach swollen and
infertile. She answers amen to this. The curse is then written down and
dissolved in the water which she accordingly drinks.

In a similar vein, both the prophet Ezekiel (Ezek. 2–3) and John, the
author of the Revelation (Rev. 10), have to eat a text, a scroll. In both
instances of semiotic metabolism, the text had a sweet taste like honey,
at the same time as the content of Ezekiel's scroll consisted of lamenta-
tions and wailings, while in the case of John the scroll turned his stomach sour. For the prophet to eat the text is then the actual internalization of the message which he is to deliver.[46] It is achieved on the same
ideal, abstract level as that of the ritual acts, but the means of getting
there is visionary rapture and not ritualization. It is interesting that the
apocalyptic genre shares the tendency toward a symbolical logic rather
than a narrative one—the symbols, for example the abstract notion of a
kingdom instantiated as a hideous beast, can act upon similar entities
without in a clear way building up a coherent narrative.

The particular ritual way of making the god or a piece of discourse
interior to the human person is in some respects also a form of interiorization of the goal of the ritual. The aim of the ritual is precisely that of
establishing something within the individual, but it also easily develops
into an interiorization of the ritual performance as in the ordeal in which
the textual liquid is supposed to either make the woman sick or not. The
decisive ritual procedure takes place within the individual.

In these forms of ritual interiorization which labor to bring about
internalization, there is a tendency of individualization which balances
the de-individualization principle of ritualization, as internalization is
the transformation of the interior of a specific individual, and not merely
the reshaping of an ideal entity.[47] The ritual thus leaves the intersubjective

---

46 An alternative way would be to burn the book and to inhale its smoke emitted from the flames.

47 Or one can as Gavin Flood (2004) in his comparative study of asceticism characterize the traditional

field and moves into the subjective realm. In the ordeal, the text enters into the woman precisely in order to make what is merely subjectively knowable intersubjective, to let the interior manifest itself in exterior signs.[48] In the same manner, the prophet eats scripture in order that he can prophesy. This interaction between interior and exterior points to an important feature of rituals, but not necessarily of ritualization, namely, that there has to be a balance between the intersubjective world of ideal entities and the interior sphere of the individual. Otherwise internalization becomes more difficult, and the individual relevance of the ritual recedes.

The constitution of the person is located at this point of intersection between public and private, and the semiotic layers of the person are bearers of the balance connecting the interior self with the social identity. It can thus seem that interiorization can be of help in the task of modeling the self, that is, of internalization, though it by no means is the only instrument of doing so. But we must also emphasize that although an identity has been established with the help of a ritual—and the individual carries with him or her traces and symbols of the new identity—it has to be maintained in everyday social and cultural life and reaffirmed by new ritual acts. In a pre-modern localized society this is not in principle a great problem, but with the advent of modernity and its insistence on the constructed and arbitrary nature of the ideal, the process meets problems of a new order and gravity.[49]

internalization as a heightened form of subjectivity, as the performance of the memory of tradition, thus distinguishing it from the self-realization of the modern individual.

48 Not surprisingly one of the first applications of advanced measurements of brain activity (brain scanning) is to detect whether a person is lying or not, not only interesting for the FBI or CIA, but also for jealous husbands or wives. A modern ordeal making the interior exterior is then created.

49 The literature on modernity and identity is large (and expanding) and ranges from general perspectives (e.g. Bauman 2000) and an abundance of studies on particular religious traditions (e.g. Brook 2006). The basic problem is that modernity as a concept has many interrelated meanings. On the one hand, it covers more material developments, such as industrialization, urbanization, and the promotion of scientific knowledge, and, on the other hand, it designates interrelated forms of ideology exemplified by enlightenment rationalism and its successors—this ideological part is perhaps more aptly designated as modernism (cf. Wallerstein [1995] who refers to a modernity of technology and a modernity of liberation). In the same way, one can distinguish between late (post) modernity and postmodernism (Woods 1999: 10).

DERITUALIZATION

According to the perspective on ritual action elaborated in this study, the particular efficacy of ritualized acts, persons, and artifacts is an effect of the fact that the abstraction achieved by ritualization provides a place for the performer in the world of ideal, abstract entities, making the person able to enter into relations with them. It is the special character of ritual semiotic action which provides voodoo ceremonies, the Christian sacraments, and royal coronations with their rationale. One can object that the gods by means of their power and will make this more mechanical logic obsolete, that the evolution from magic to religion is a development away from the belief in impersonal laws, instead turning to the supplication of supernatural persons. However, in most religions also the gods are subject to this semiotics; it is the natural laws of their ideal world, the operating principles of myth. And to abandon that form of reasoning is, then, not necessarily an elimination of magic, but entails instead a process of deritualization, although complete a-ritualism is perhaps not possible for humans, at least as long there is a need to act upon abstract principles in public.

When, for example, the moral status of the ritual participant is made into a condition of ritual efficacy, this could be introduced as a necessary but not sufficient condition—without inner purity ritual sanctification is futile. An inner defilement annuls all ritual labor, making it at heart fruitless or even detrimental. At the same time, purity in itself is still considered as insufficient for achieving the regeneration or transformation wished for in the ritual. But when purity is seen as a sufficient condition of, for example, deification, then two means are available to achieve the same goal. Within a tradition this can lead to a division between the order of ascetics and mystics who seek purity by extreme regimens and on the other hand the majority of believers who still foremost put their trust in ritual activity. A tradition can also on a larger scale move away from rituals and put increasing emphasis on, for example, moral behavior. The same can be said about the other forms of interiorization of ritual efficacy such as feelings, knowledge, and spiritual qualities. We must, nevertheless, discuss intentionality in a little more detail as we have—following Humphrey and Laidlaw—defined ritualization as the "giving up" of individual intentionality.

The peculiar quality adhering to the act of giving intentionality importance for ritual efficacy is grounded in this form of interiorization seeming to stand in a logical opposition to ritualization itself. In actions done according to some form of instrumental rationality, there is a close connection between the purpose of the action and the intention. The intention is the will to perform a certain type of action which is chosen as it is conducive to a particular desired end. The purpose is, therefore, often built into the categorization of the act, the description of it, as in the case of murder. The same act done according to another purpose is hence categorized as self-defense, neutralizing the enemy or execution. But all these acts could also more neutrally be categorized as merely killing a person, leaving the question of specific intention more open. The often intimate connection between intention and purpose becomes more complex when we consider series of acts each having their immediate purpose, while they at the same time function as links in a chain fashioned in accordance with an overarching purpose: in this way, human life could be analyzed as consisting of chains of actions held together by higher-level purposes ultimately grounded in some basic motives. Similarly, most actions, as a murder or a drive home, could be dissolved into minor moments each requiring a separate act of the will or being merely activated by a prior more conscious movement of the will (cf. the virtual intention); it would be very cumbersome if every little bodily movement required an explicit act of the will. Major decisions that depend upon the weighing of alternative ways of action in distinction benefit from a higher degree of discursive reasoning. Everyday life then moves along helped by many more or less automatic actions done by routine or guided by passions overpowering both will and reason—life unfolding according to habit, passion, and reason in different proportions. This is basically a description of life guided by instrumental rationality with some obvious constraints, but when we introduce normative rationality into the picture this order is changed. Then actions become carried out not primarily because we want to achieve a certain purpose, but because we consider the norms as binding. This could ultimately be based upon tradition in the sense that "this is the way we have always done it," on supernatural origin, as in "this is the word of God," the nature of the universe, or reason itself. However, norms mostly do not in detail regulate individual behavior, but the norms of a social group define the legitimate space for instrumental rationality that is available for an individual. There are many types of norms as moral rules defining acts as good or bad, etiquette distinguishing between what is proper and improper, laws governing many areas of human life deciding whether they are legal or criminal and thus deserving of punishment or not.

Ritual norms constitute a special category as they do not only decide whether the action is good, legal, or proper, that is, within the category of legitimate actions, but aim at the transformation of action itself by a special high degree of normativity. When an action has been ritualized there is almost no room for individual instrumental rationality, the intention (i.e. the category of the act) is socially defined as, for example, a sacrifice or a baptism. However, ritual acts are constrained by other sets of norms; with other words, they must fall within the limits of legitimate action. For example, in most modern societies the ritual killing of human persons is both illegal and considered immoral. Ritual norms thus differ from legal and moral norms, which potentially cover all actions, considering the same actions from different perspectives, focusing on their legal or moral character. We can also consider other norms, for example aesthetical, which decide the degree of beauty of the ritual acts, but which do not in an immediate way place them within or outside the limits of legitimate action—if ugly rituals are not prohibited. Ritual norms are invalid outside of the ritually created boundaries, but within them they are of course used as guidelines for deciding which actions are correct and which are incorrect; this distinction could be connected to the legal system, thereby making the transgression of a ritual prescription a legal offence.

Moreover, ritual action is not only embedded in a wider context of normative systems regulating legitimate action, but as in our picture of life as consisting horizontally of chains of actions and vertically of an order of purposes, ritual acts are embedded and constrained by higher order purposes and motives. Beside the wider context of normative rationality, one therefore must also consider the two-dimensional picture of instrumental rationality. In this way, we arrive at the question of the relation between normative and instrumental rationality in the case of rituals.

In contrast to legal norms which in principle constrain all actions, ritual norms are more specific and intensive, and ritual actions can, therefore, become embedded in a chain of non-ritual actions. The ritual itself perhaps must be performed, giving the individual no real choice, but it can become a building block in rather different life projects. For example, the Christian sacrament of confirmation could for someone religiously devout be a ritual used in order to achieve inclusion in his or her church, while for another more nominal Christian this is a ritual marking the transition into adult life: the next time this individual sets foot in church it is for the funeral, which only in a secondary way could be said to be the individual's action.

This instrumental use of rituals attains another level of intensity when the ritual is optional. There could exist in a premodern society a spectrum of legitimate ritual choices, but the purpose is then mostly built into the ritual. If you want a child, do this one, if you want rain, do that one, etc. In our globalized and secularized world, the scoop for choice is much wider. One could shop rituals on the global market, thus becoming a customer who moves along shelves filled with spectacular rites picking and choosing according to one's need, taste, or whims. Nevertheless, such an instrumental use of rituals as commodities still treats them as objects. When entering into the chosen ritual, ritual normativity has to take the place of instrumental reasoning. There are many ways to achieve fame besides doing a particular ritual designed for that purpose, but if one starts to indulge in these alternative means during the ritual, the abstract nature of the ritual person will be weakened or destroyed.

The interiorization of the intention, the ritual commitment, entails a movement away from the social stipulation of the act, that is, ritualization itself and the de-individualized character that it confers on actions. At the same time, it makes the individual's understanding of the act crucial. The categorization of the ritual is then dependent upon some interior act, which when lacking renders the ritual not merely inefficacious, but undermines its essence; it is not an action of the type desired at all. We can see some of this tendency in the difference between the Catholic position on the nature of baptism and the Pentecostal understanding of the baptism in the Holy Spirit. Though ultimately deriving its efficacy from the Holy Spirit, the Catholic understanding of the baptism relies upon a ritual action logic in which the criteria for a successful ritual are exterior. The baptism with (in, of) the Holy Spirit in a Pentecostal tradition is, on the other hand, eminently an interior act, an actual experience of the Holy Spirit, without that element it would not be a baptism in the Holy Spirit at all, but instead falls within a totally different category. The Catholic understanding of baptism and confirmation does not rule out this sort of experiences, but does not make the ritual dependent upon them. At the same time, the interior experience of the baptism in the Holy Spirit has to manifest itself in order to be socially significant—with the importance of, for example, glossolalia then becoming decisive:

> Of all the pastoral concerns at the Azusa Mission, none was of greater importance than the issue of precisely how to know if one had truly received the sought-after baptism with the Holy Ghost and fire. In many ways this was the pentecostal question. Of all the wonderful experiences of the Holy Spirit one might have, how was the baptism of the Spirit to be distinguished from the others? … The problem had always been how to know what precisely marked this experience as unique. Parham's great contribution in this regard—which was also the first and most significant pentecostal answer to the question— had been to suggest that speaking in other tongues was the sign that infallibly distinguished the baptism of the Spirit from all other works of God in the human heart. Parham asserted quite bluntly that if one did not have the biblical evidence of speaking in tongues, one had not received a true baptism of the Spirit. (Jacobsen 2003: 74)

Such an externalization of the interior can become more or less ritual in character, for example, when the speaking in tongues follows stereotyped patterns of behavior (cf. Holm 1987). But this is a secondary ritualization of the interiorization of the intention; in its primary movement, it has great potential for deritualization with its focus on the individual and his or her interior mental life.

When we consider the interiorization of the purpose or motive of a ritual act, it is not primarily the understanding of the category of action that is in question. Instead, the decisive importance given to interior purpose or motive activates instrumental rationality within the domain of normative rationality. Suddenly, it is not only the following of the ritual norm that matters, but what goals that are being pursued by the ritual practitioner. This could take many forms. One of them is to treat the goals wished for in accordance with a moral framework, as the goals are often extra-ritual. For example, to perform a ritual in order to impress one's fellow beings with one's wealth and magnanimous spirit ultimately motivated by vanity could be deemed morally bad, while to perform the ritual in order to please the god is considered as morally good. However, one can use a similar strategy within a tradition and dissuade the ritual performers to have any extra-ritual purposes at all, instead insisting on a disinterested attitude focused on keeping up ritualization. In such a case, the stoic resignation in lieu of the fruits of the action is made into the crucial point of ritual efficacy, without which ritual acts are pointless.

The decisive problem with insisting on, for example, a morally bad purpose destroying the efficacy of the ritual is how one is to decide what the purpose of the individual is—to lay bare his or her motives. There is a difference between, on the one hand, actions done according to a specific purpose that mostly fit into a chain of instrumentally motivated actions, and, on the other hand, ritual actions which by their high degree of normativity are disconnected from that chain. The interiorization of the purpose is then an attempt to individualize the action—to insist on the ritual act being situated in a context of instrumental thinking—but this does not automatically result in a difference in exterior behavior; the purpose is hence hidden in the interior. This could lead to the social pre-occupation with signs of intentionality becoming activated, and the purpose becomes ritually constructed: "What do you wish for?," "I wish…" Or one could use forms of divination or ordeals.

However, the great deritualizing potential lies in the focus being moved to, for example, morality instead of ritual. Moral uprightness becomes then the sole criterion for efficaciously dealing with the ideal realm, entailing a movement away from a preoccupation with sacralization, turning instead toward holiness built up by morally good actions. This difference is typified in the relation between the office of the priest and that of the holy man or woman.

At the same time, it must be emphasized that ritual traditions have to devote energy to the desires of individuals, to the purposes and motives of everyday instrumentally oriented life as health, wealth, and glory. However, these must not be considered as decisive for the efficacy of the ritual, but can be given prominence within the ritual, such as the desire for cattle in a pastoral society. This changes somewhat when we move from considering the interiorization of the efficacy of the ritual to the interiorization of its effects, that is, the goal of the ritual. But though the goal is portrayed as eminently interior, as the increasing of some inner energy instead of gaining an abundance of cattle, this does not in the same way as the interiorization of ritual efficacy lend itself to deritualization—that is, if not a more powerful means of achieving the same goal is presented. The interiorization of the effects of the ritual is actually one way in which interiorization helps to turn the attention within a ritual context toward the individual. The ritual becomes relevant for the life of the individual, as when it focuses on interior healing, cancelling of sin, and the increasing of self-respect. If, however, the faith in the efficacy of the ritual is lacking then this individual relevance vaporizes, and religious ceremonies become mere stereotyped behavior.

Interior performance—the carrying out of a ritual inside the mind or the body—is not always merely dealing with the physical body, in a modern understanding of it, but concerns the manipulation of a subtle body which is both physical and psychical, thinly material. If visualizations and silent prayers combined with exterior postures and movements are performed according to ritual norms, this is not a great threat to ritualization as such. When the performance is exterior, the ritual space is viewed as a field of meaning, a world of abstract entities made present by sacralized symbols. When the performance is interior, this field of ideal entities and the ritual action affecting them take place within the body—the gods as well as the virtues are then located within the body. This could be very helpful for internalization, the process of making ideal entities part of the self: they are all placed within the person and act upon each other inside the body. However, the transposing of the inter-subjective ideal world into the subjective interior of the individual makes the social dimension of ritual activity problematic. That is, if this introjection of the abstract entities into the subjective sphere of the person develops into the main ritual activity, then it brings with it a weakening of the force of ritualization. This challenge increases when the interior ritual becomes detached from an exterior ritual frame and transposed to the non-ritual life of instrumental actions. Ritual then fades into the category of prayer and meditation, perhaps merely providing a general mindfulness to ordinary actions.

The potential for deritualization by interiorization, however, reaches its peak when all three dimensions of ritual action are interiorized. The act is then performed in the interior, its goal is interior, and its efficacy is completely derived from interior principles. In this way, ritual has no real relevance outside of the individual, the very opposite of hyper-ritualization. But the final link still attaching this interior ritual to intersubjective ritual norms is severed by individualism, when the individual takes upon itself to decide when or how to perform the interior ritual—in which case the the ritual commitment dies and deritualization moves toward its completion.

CHAPTER FOUR

Modernity and Deritualization

In the previous chapter, it was indicated that ritual interiorization in certain situations can be part of a movement away from ritual; either particular forms of ritual or ritual in itself. Such discourses and practices of ritual criticism have emerged in various time periods, but most conspicuously as a result of the protestant reformation that gave individual interiority a new authority at the expense of the ecclesial structure with its elaborate system of rituals. However, it is not an irreversible development to which, for example, the ritualization within the Methodist Church in the nineteenth century testifies. Such a re-ritualization, though, must grapple with a strong foundational ideology of interiorization, as shown by the quotation below. It is the interior man, the spirit, which should be in focus, if one is not to fall into the trap of ritualism, which signifies an occupation with exterior features at the expense of interiority:

As might be expected, not all Methodists were enamored of this shift. Efforts were made to calm the anxieties of those who saw the promotion of Christian festal days as one more intrusion of formality and ritualism. In *A Treatise on the Lenten Season*, Bostwick Hawley argued that in addition to "giving some needed instruction to the people," "a judicious observance of these anniversaries would induce a reform in extreme ritualistic Churches." Another writer who claimed that Methodism had "not rejected a moderate use . . . of commemorative days" and testified to the "almost universal" celebration of Christmas and Easter in churches in the eastern half of the country nevertheless insisted that caution be taken "lest in the ceremonial we lose sight of the spirit that underlies, and lest by a multiplication of days we return to what the Church found it necessary to abandon." (Tucker 2001: 51)

In a context that puts great value on interiority, the concept and process of ritualization thus acquires as ritualism a pejorative character, which should not blind us to the fact that for the most part varieties of interiorization and ritualization coexist rather peacefully. For example, the word "ritualism" is used in the English translation of Benedict XVI's Post-Synodal Apostolic Exhortation *Sacramentum Caritatis*, that is, in a text very much advocating an ethos of emotionally restrained liturgy emphasizing the aesthetical qualities of impersonal ritual acts. The ritual perfectly performed, but without the desired interior elements, is, nevertheless, described as falling into "ritualism":

> For this reason, the Synod of Bishops asked that the faithful be helped to make their interior dispositions correspond to their gestures and words. Otherwise, however carefully planned and executed our liturgies may be, they would risk falling into a certain ritualism. (Benedict XVI 2007)

This can be compared with the animated defense of "ritualism" by the anthropologist Mary Douglas in her book *Natural Symbols* (1996 [1970]) which was written in the context of the revolutionary late 1960s and the liturgical reforms in the wake of the second Vatican council. She does not advocate ritual formalism for its own sake though, but defends rituals as such under the banner of ritualism against the anti-ritualism of the prevailing zeitgeist. She chastises the trend toward deritualization which she explicitly connects to interiorization:

> Let me use this excerpt to signpost three phases in the move away from ritualism. First, there is the contempt of external ritual forms; second, there is the private internalizing of religious experience; third, there is the move to humanist philanthropy. When the third stage is under way, the symbolic life of the spirit is finished. (Douglas 1996 [1970]: 7)

The use of "ritualism" as a rhetorical tool has to be connected to the wider discourse in which interiorization is seen as inimical to ritual practice, either in a pro-ritual way as Mary Douglas, or in the manner of a pro-choice criticism of ritual, in which individual conscience takes the front row. This tension between interiority and deference to social authority is often connected to the transition from a premodern (ritualist) mindset to a modern subjectivity characterized by a high degree of interior reflexivity—a theme, for example, surfacing in the following analysis of the romantic understanding of Hamlet as a typical modern hero:

> As Kerrigan convincingly shows, the romantic Hamlet assumes a generative distinction between ancient and modern. Anthropologically speaking, this difference was presented as a transition from an ethical system based on collective ritual to one based on the interiority of the modern subject. Hegel's analysis of Hamlet is exemplary of the romantic critical enterprise as a whole. Whereas a classical hero like Oedipus is destined to suffer for crimes he is totally ignorant of, the romantic Hamlet suffers because he internalizes as a representation—for example, in the figure of the ghost, the player's speech, and the Mousetrap play—the crimes his uncle has committed. For the classical hero, torment comes from without; at the end of the play, Oedipus is ritually banished for transgressing taboos (parricide and incest) that preexist his capacity to understand or control them. For the modern hero, torment comes from within; haunted by the memory of his father's death, Hamlet invents fictional scenes by which he attempts to relieve himself of his ethical duty to revenge. For Hegel, as indeed for most moderns, this internalization of the classical scene of collective sacrifice is considered an ethical advance. (Oort 2006: 322–23)

In *Ritual and its Consequences* (2008), by Adam Seligman (religious studies), Robert Weller (anthropology), Michael Puett (sinology), and Bennet Simon (psychoanalysis), the anti-ritual stance of modernity is thematized as a variant on the conflict between a sincere and a ritual mode of behavior. The latter is characterized by the creation of a playful world indulging in an as-if attitude in which the imperfect nature of human life is acknowledged, boundaries created and toyed with, both recognizing them and challenging them. This subjunctive, illusory world created by ritual is in fact the social, cultural space of a group. The sincere mode, on the other hand, privileges the as-is dimension and constitutes a movement away from the shared subjunctive world to what is authentic and really real, which ultimately is the inner self. Sincerity resents ambiguity and wants to either establish clear-cut borders or abolish them completely—an attitude leading quite naturally to utopian social projects. These two modes are presented as Weberian ideal types and are thus present in different degrees in all societies; examples are taken from ancient China and Judaism, but the prime examples of the sincere mode are Protestantism and enlightenment modernity. Sincerity with a capital S is hence, in the terminology of this study, a form of ritual interiorization when still acknowledging ritual performance as legitimate, but when it doesn't, it has left the ritual sphere in order to construct alternative, more sincere modes of handling life. It is, however, important to emphasize that the sincere mode is not coextensive with interiorization—it does not cover the whole spectrum of ritual interiorization, but Seligman and his co-authors have delineated with this notion a pervasive tendency within modernity which, however, is not always explicitly concerned with ritual.

> Indeed, the entire world of liberal modernity can be usefully understood in terms of the tropes of sincerity. The centrality of the individual and the valuation of the private are after all central to the normative program of liberal, enlightened modernity. From this follows modernity's extremely discursive character, its cultural stress on the unique and singular, and in this country anyway, its privileging of individual choice above repetitive action. (Seligman et al. 2008: 118)

Their analysis of modernity can be used as a tool to lay bare some more or less unacknowledged premises inherent in secular, post-protestant studies of, for example, religion—alerting us to misrepresentations and hidden default value judgments. However, also their study is thoroughly and explicitly normative in that they maintain that "[o]nly through a reengagement with ritual as a constitutive aspect of the human project will it be possible to negotiate the emergent realities of our present century" (2008: 10). Their critique of modernity—both in its hard boundary-affirming aspect and in its liberal boundary-abolishing aspect combined with their praise of ritual practice—opens up for the charge that they want to reestablish premodern forms of religiosity. Consequently, they energetically reject fundamentalism as a dangerous case of the sincere mode, which in this way is defined as a typically modern project.[50] Ritual, on the other hand, is a way for global social life to move forward beyond modernism, postmodernism, and religious fanaticism. It is the playful nature of ritual that they affirm—that which both acknowledges the reality of natural life and social structure, trying out these and alternatives to them in a mode of suspended disbelief. Ritual in the hands of the authors of *Ritual and its Consequences* is invested with liberating power, in contrast to the use of "ritualism" in other discourses to indicate the sterility of such activity.

Though their analysis of the sincere mode is helpful by presenting as an ideal type a complex phenomenon, it obscures the ways in which the various forms of interiorization and ritualization coexist and interact. The sincere mode is used to signify an interconnected larger set of strategies, a comprehensive ideology, especially in its modernist form, which is depicted as inherently anti-ritualist. The problem is that they do not attempt to delineate subcategories of sincerity, which leads to the dichotomy at times becoming too simple, to which one must add a consideration of the normative dimension inscribed in their taxonomy. For even if we were to subscribe to the redemptive nature of ritual as such, it is not always so in real life, and then these aberrations have to be designed as inauthentic renderings, perverted manifestations of what essentially is good, as in the case of fundamentalist rituals. The focus is for obvious

---

50 The tricky thing, though, is that liberal changes to traditional religiosity in which sincerity is used as a mode of arguing (for example, women priests and gay bishops) are considered as "expressions of creativity" (Seligman et al. 2008: 127) in distinction to sincere fundamentalism which is a "dangerous form of religious sentimentality" (126). The crucial difference seems to be that fundamentalists try to impose religious ideals on secular society, while the liberal reforms work in the opposite direction.

reasons transferred from ritual to its context. Nazi meetings were extensively and effectively ritualized, and to argue that they were inauthentic rituals is not to point to deficiencies in their ritual performance, but to the larger worldview that they were part of. Labeling such rituals as sincere is then not to invest goodness in ritualization *per se*, but in a special mode of ritual and extra-ritual activity which is more playful (postmodern) than rigid (modern).

Another difference is that their characterization of ritualization, though in several ways overlapping with that of this study, differs in significant aspects. First, they focus on play and fiction, while I have chosen to highlight abstraction as the basic process giving ritualization its fundamental character. When choosing the theme of play, ritual activity is linked to the imagination while the sincere mode, on the other hand, is directed toward what really is—and hence reason. The conflict is consequently between fiction (ritual) and fact (sincerity). The question is why the subjunctive social world of ritual is not seen as real in the first place. Why is the hidden interiority of the individual more real and important than intersubjective norms and authority? And is there not also within modernity an equally strong current striving toward the abolishment of man—to the collectivism of a Brave New World? Modernity is Janus-faced in containing both currents of humanism and those of post- or anti-humanism. In order to proceed in our discussion of the relation between modernity and interiority and thus deritualization, it is high time to reconnect to the process of abstraction chosen in this study as foundational for ritual activity.

NOMINALISM

Modernity at least in its more ideological versions carries with it a major impetus toward the subjective and hence individualism, the very opposite of the ritual commitment (cf. Taylor 2002, Ferguson 2000: 198). But deeper still, I maintain that nominalism is the basic feature of modernity, which inclines it toward deritualization. Nominalism signifies a stance according to which only the individual has being and the ideal realm in the form of notions and norms is in reality merely made up of

more or less arbitrary[51] collections of particulars (conceptual nominalism) and acts of will on the part of individuals (voluntarism). In such a
demythologized universe, the action logic of religious rituals becomes
absurd, or has to be interpreted as merely expressive actions in order to
salvage the rationality of the ritual practitioner. The affirmation of ritual
practice by Seligman et al. is set in such a nominalist context. The ideal
realm is one of illusion, of fiction, though viewed as something positive, as a way to creatively handle the realities of natural and social life,
negotiating ways to act within the constraints set upon human existence.
Consequently, their endorsement of ritualization constitutes not a return
to an enchanted realist mode in which the ideal realm is more real than
the profane everyday world, but an argument for the continued relevance
of ritual in a modern context.

To pinpoint nominalism in this sense as the major feature of modernity undermining ritual semiotics is also simultaneously to advocate
a history of modernity which locates its birth in the late Middle Ages.
There is a substantial body of scholarship that makes this connection.
Louis Dupré, for example, in his book *Passage to Modernity* states:

> Only when the early humanist notion of human creativity came to
> form a combustive mixture with the negative conclusions of nomi-
> nalist theology did it cause the cultural explosion that we refer to as
> modernity. It shattered the organic unity of the Western view of the
> real. ... Whereas previously meaning had been established in the very
> act of creation by a wise God, it now fell upon the human mind to
> interpret cosmos, the structure of which had ceased to be given as
> intelligible. Instead of being an integral part of the cosmos, the person
> became its source of meaning. (Dupré 1993: 3)

The nominalist inclination within modernity transforms abstraction
from an adventure of discovery, of climbing ever higher on the ladder of

---

51 The level of arbitrariness depends upon how radical the nominalism espoused is; ranging from the
    denial of concepts (merely *nomen*) to conceptualism.

being, to an act of construction on the part of the individual. The individual arranges reality according to schemas of its own; it is not the world that reveals itself to the human intellect. A fallacy inspiring fear and drawing grave reproach is consequently reification, in which the creations of the subject are given the ontological status of an individual. In a religious context, the opposite is frequently the case. Truth is not merely a quality of statements, their verification or falsification, but also, for example, as in Christianity when a person comes to the fore when Jesus declares that "I am the truth." Human moral and legal norms are also often considered as merely the pale reflection of the eternal law. [52] Religion builds on the belief in the reality of the abstract, in this way combining metaphysics with the powers of the imagination. This also affects religious narrative, such as myths, as they too rely on conceptual realism—the idea that concepts, for example wisdom, exist apart from human thinking, on a plane of higher order than everyday life. Mythical figures thus act according to the same logic which undergirds ritual action. We could say that myth in the form of narrative represents actions on the level of the ideal, while rituals concretely act these out, though not in a narrative form, but in the typical formal way of abstract action. There is thus no chicken-and-egg-problem when dealing with myth and ritual—both base themselves on the same process, that of abstraction. The basic religious position is a far reaching realism and personification, though it is important to note that nominalism in the late Middle Ages emerged as a theological position. Modernity has thus theological roots; it can actually be read as the result of certain theological positions, as grappling with theological questions in a particular form, but containing within itself the departure from religion (cf. Brient 2002: 61–73; Gillespie 2008).

Interiorization is sometimes connected to the nominalist tendency of modernity, its disbelief in the reality of abstract entities. Interiorization then becomes a way of turning the ritual toward what has being (cf. Ferguson 2000: 190). In this process, the surface of the person is not satisfactory, as this is the semiotic layer anchoring the individual in both

52 Cf. the pre-existent Torah and Koran, e.g. Sawyer 1999: 105; Rippin 1993: 104.

the intersubjective realm and in the interior. If the intersubjective world loses its higher grade of reality, then the surface of the person becomes demythologized—it becomes skin and in order to find the really real, one must turn toward the subjective realm and the idiosyncratic. In this process, personhood loses its connection to the notion of individual, as the abstract notion of person does not have a being of its own; the individual is not an instance of this universal, a concretization of it, but the notion "person" becomes instead a more or less arbitrary collection of originals. The individual loses personhood and becomes a subject, a consciousness, a mere point in space-time. And as having shed the abstract, it has also discarded meaning; all social roles become now mere texture to the surface of the individual who lacks intrinsic nature other than consciousness: it is hence only the emperor as an individual in the modern sense that can lose his clothes and be exposed as naked, as having skin without semiotic value. In Buddhist thinking, on the other hand, both a Buddha and a cakravartin, a world ruler, have thirty-two special signs; for example, their foot soles are smooth and inscribed with the wheel of dharma, their fingers are very long and connected with a thin web, and their bodily hair is growing upwards.[53] To unrobe the Buddha would hence not reveal nakedness in the sense of raw flesh without semiotic value, but would uncover a body extraordinarily full of refulgent meaning.

INTERIORIZATION IN A WIDER SENSE

Throughout this book, the discussion has been centered on religious rituals, moving from the theme of interiorization and exteriorization to that of deritualization—the tense relationship between ritualization and interiorization. As a final note, I would like to indicate an even wider context for processes of interiorization, in that way opening up avenues for interdisciplinary research, or at least communication. Ritualization, though in many ways special, shares basic traits with other types of normative rationality. There are—besides ritual traditions—moral, legal, and aesthetical normative systems, and in all of these the same type of

53 The thirty-two signs are enumerated in Lakkhana Sutta.

focus on the interior could emerge in different degrees, either on the level of discourse or on that of practice.[54] For example, in jurisprudence or in the courtroom, there could arise a view that the intention of the act under consideration resides primarily in the interior. The judge and the jury, consequently, probe the exterior for signs of this crucial interior intention. The opposite position, in a manner similar to ritualization, considers the act, for example a murder, as socially stipulated, its nature deriving from its performance. In the first case, the exterior is treated as a medium bearing signs of the interior, while, in the second case, interiority is seen as embodied, as residing in the exterior action and its social context (Duff 1990; Cavallin 1999).

An interiorized view of morality, in a similar vein, makes the exterior part of action insignificant for deciding whether an act is good or bad. The goodness resides, according to such a position, solely in the intentionality or feelings of the one acting.[55] As always when the crucial element is hidden, either a search for signs is undertaken, or as in this case morality becomes subjective, in the sense of residing within the hidden depths of the individual. Interiorization in the sphere of morality can then in analogy to ritual interiorization assist in abolishing the notion of an intersubjective morality founded on objective features.

In aesthetics, the same process emerges: the work of art does not become what it is by virtue of intersubjective criteria, the norms regulating the production and estimation of artistic artifacts. On the contrary, the nature of art resides in the interior of the artist—there is no work of art without it and with it anything could turn out to be art. But without criteria (norms) for beauty, the sublime or for any other supreme value defining the artistic work and its reception, the interior of the artist, his or her intentionality, perhaps combined with a non-discursive intuition,

---

54 In order to be "alive," a normative system must of course always constitute a practice, as in the case of languages; such forms of life can through discourse become reflexively aware of their own normativity and instigate initiatives for the regulation and delimitation of practice, e.g., books of grammar; though this never amounts to an abolishment of the normative processes operating on the level of practice.

55 For a discussion of moral relativism, see Levy 2002.

becomes the only real work of art.[56] The life, actions, and utterances of the artist are thus scrutinized for evidence of this interior essence of art, but it always retains its elusive character, though it is constantly under pressure to externalize, to establish new sets of norms for artistic work and evaluation. In order to be true to the underlying theme of interiorization, the artist must then constantly intercept this process, and in an iconoclastic temper destroy his own creation when it is threatened by reification.

And, in all this, it is difficult not to perceive a profile of modernity emerging which presses toward the interior in search of the really real and a secure foundation for knowledge, but becomes frustrated by the elusive nature of the hidden and subjective (see e.g. Bowie 2003). The pendulum moves then to the other extreme point, that is, the attempt to abolish the interior in the wish of making everything exterior, and when an interior makes itself noticed through the cracks of the surface of the monistic worldview, the pendulum inevitably moves back (cf. Jay 1996). It moves from idealism to materialism as the affirmation of the reality of the ideal, of the intersubjective realm, is beyond its reach due to its basic nominalism, the foundation of the *via moderna*. Between consciousness and nature it is bound to move, like Sisyphus who, according to Camus (1942), is a characteristically modern hero in his futile toil, the ultimate reward for his cunning.

We can see this oscillating movement also within religious studies, and more broadly in the humanities and social sciences. The dialectics of modernism and postmodernism guiding research within these fields is colored by the recourse to the subject with an ensuing idealism accord-

---

56 The same way of interiorizing the nature of art could instead of devoting its energy to the interior of the artist argue that the artfulness of art resides in the eye of the beholder. To be a work of art it must be seen as such by the audience. The creative act is hence taken away from the artistic genius, everybody being artists, but, in the same manner, the intention of the art work resides in their interior—a tremendous burden laid on the shoulders of the public. An exteriorizing version of this move is to leave the definition of what is art and what is not to institutions such as academies, museums, and galleries. There is, then, no objective quality residing in the object that decides its inclusion in, or exclusion from, the category of art, neither is the evaluation on the part of the individual spectator relevant, but the judgment is left completely to the contingent stipulative definitions made by art institutions. What is exhibited at the gallery is art by definition.

ing to which the mind creates wholly or partly the world. At the same
time, the elusive nature of the interior manifests itself in the erosion of
the subject, the flight is then to language, to the intersubjective in the
form of discourse, but this is only ephemeral, as discourse is always
constructed, thus directing the gaze toward the constructor in search
for something more real and prior in a causal sense. The postmodern
struggle with the empowering but ultimately claustrophobic (subjectiv-
ist) nature of idealism is now within religious studies losing territory to
a cognitive paradigm, which, contrary to what most scholars who have
been influenced by the postmodern criticism of grand narratives deemed
possible, constitutes a resurrection of a heroic modernity as a post-post-
modernism (cf. Bell 2006). The cognitivist is also focused on the mind,
but for him (or more seldom, for her) there is no real interior, everything
is at least potentially exterior, the basic tenet of naturalism, the guiding
a priori assumption.

For the postmodernist, the individual is merely a nodal point of the
discursive processes, a particular density of narrative. Although the body
is often in the analytical focus, it is chiefly as being plastic to the will of
the mind and the structure of discourse—its physicality like prime matter is merely a potentiality, not a substrate. For the cognitivist, on the
other hand, individuality resides in the material brain. The intersubjective world of culture, meaning, and language is merely electric states in
particular brains. Though these two positions (idealism and materialism) on the scale that modern man has to walk in his quest to understand himself are located at the extreme ends of his ideological oscilla-
tion, they are both dependent on a basic nominalism and a consequent
skepticism. This is acknowledged by the cognitivist Ilkka Pyysiäinen in
his book *How Religion Works:*

> Although "postmodernism" and cognitive science are two completely
> different systems of thought, they here converge, in the sense that cog-
> nitive scientists such as Varela, Rosch and Thompson (1996: 198–217,
> 231–33), and (with some reservations) Clark (1997: 83–102), have for

example emphasized the relational, i.e. non-absolute nature of such concepts as 'self' and 'world.' Neither concept can provide an ultimate ground for ethics or for anything else, both of them being conditioned by the natural drift of evolution. The difference between postmodernism and cognitive science is that cognitive scientists accept the process of evolution as a truly explanatory factor. Neither the external world nor cognition is taken as a fixed given, both being viewed as co-evolving systems without any ultimate ground. The human cognitive system is an emergent outcome of the self-organization of matter; external reality is perceived in the way it is because evolution has shaped the human perceptual system to be such as it is. Organisms and environment enfold into each other and unfold from one another. (Pyysiäinen 2003: 164)

The same point is made by Gerard Delanty in his discussion of modernity and postmodernity which connects them through the common theme of skepticism, which eventually turns toward the subject:

[P]ostmodernity is also a continuation of the modern project, which must be seen as one of radical scepticism, the penetration of scepticism into the identity of the self. What is coming to an end today is postmodernity in so far as this has construed itself as the successor of modernity. Postmodernity can no longer claim the mantle of scepticism for itself, for, as I have argued, this is part of the modern itself ... Postmodernity is better understood as a deepening of the reflexive and sceptical moment of the modern itself. If modernity was a critique of objectivity in the name of a self-legislating subjectivity who becomes the order of all things, postmodernity can be seen as a dissolution of this very subjectivity. (Delanty 2000: 5)

The cognitivist thus has to face the dilemma between, on the one hand, the great trust that the achievements of the natural sciences inspire and, on the other hand, the disheartening insight that science has no view from outside, that rationality operates not according to timeless principles, but is merely an eccentric outcome of genetic variation.

The underlying metaphysics of religious ritual and mythology decisively differ on this point and this explains the demythologizing ethos of modernity both in its idealist and materialist versions. When trying to forge interdisciplinary links based on a common theme of interiorization, this basic feature of modernity will inevitably become an issue, if not openly recognized, then in more implicit ways.

Furthermore, ritualization through being an intense form of normativity can make its appearance in any type of normative rationality. Morality can thus, when starting to regulate life in increasing detail, more and more limit the scope of instrumental reasoning to the extreme end, when all actions in their minute details are considered as either good or bad—always leaving merely one option to pursue if the person does not want to fall into sin. This extreme form is, however, unlivable, that is, if it does not allow for exceptions, such as the rabbinical solution to the prohibition of not traveling more than a certain distance during the Sabbath by placing a water bottle under the seat, as there is a special rule for traveling over water, or the special Shabbat elevators that stop at each story so there is no need to press any button.[57]

But even though the ritualistic nature of such a circumstantial moral code is evident, it still has not the same strong relation to the nature of semiotic action which is characteristic for religious rituals, though we should expect the precepts to move from a legal to a moral and a religious sphere quite effortlessly in such cases as the highly regulated life of an ultra-orthodox Jew. However, also a purely secular moral system can develop in the same ritualistic vein. The belief in the reality of the ideal is then absent and the result is more in the nature of an automatized life. And if we exchange moral goodness and badness for the modern notion of efficiency and let the decision of what is efficient reside in the higher echelons of an organization, we get the peculiar ritual nature of the efficient worker and bureaucrat. We could also consider the ritual nature of

---

57 For a whole book devoted to evasions of the Sabbath law, see Dundes 2002.

war, the de-individualizing of the soldier, the solemn ritual treatment of the flag, the symbol of the nation, and the central position of the hero—the ideal soldier—and so forth. But if modern warfare still retains many ritual elements, it is, nevertheless, more focused on efficiency, and the ritual elements can be retained mainly for their practical import.

Once again we are led to a consideration of modernity and now to its characteristic feature of functional differentiation which points to a decisive difference between premodern and modern societies. The process of differentiation suggests that in premodern societies moral, legal, and ritual norms and domains interpenetrate or form a more or less seamless whole. The ritualized nature of warfare then quite naturally takes on a religious dimension, and, which is also the case in modern societies, a legal and a moral nature. Consequently, if we from a modern viewpoint would consider the ritualization and interiorization of legal and moral normative systems as in principle independent of each other, in a premodern mindset, for which functional differentiation has not taken on the great importance it has for us, ritualization and interiorization provide natural points of fusion or linkage between these types of norms, and the behavior they regulate.

On the other hand, the modern vision of morality as divorced from the law and the sphere of religious rituals is hardly practical in its extreme form. Mostly, a hierarchical order of norms is provided as when rituals are constrained by legal norms, for example in the use of the Sikh dagger kirpan, but this is not a static phenomenon. The return of the sacred could press even secular societies to make concessions to religious and ritual norms on a legal level. The secular order turned on its head in this way is exemplified by the modern Iranian theocracy in which religious authorities constitute the supreme normative authority, for example through The Guardian Council of the Constitution (Mir-Hosseini 2006: 18).

The dominant tendency of the global capitalist system is to provide material for the current consumerist lifestyle, thus giving instrumental rationality increasing importance at the expense of normative rationality. The ideal state of things for people embracing this development is a world society without any norms that restrict desire and the efforts to satisfy it; these instead efficiently structure human life by their own inherent natures—achieving temporary equilibriums. An interdisciplinary investigation of interiorization is inevitably situated in this context. It has to move its focus to and fro, from the modern condition to the premodern and then back again to the postmodern realization that any such dealing with anthropology, of what a human person is and could be, cannot fail to direct the searchlight also to his or her own *a priori* assumptions of what constitutes human nature or the lack of such an essence.

Bibliography

Adler, Joseph A. 2002. *Chinese Religions.* London: Routledge.

Adler, Margot. 1986 [1979]. *Drawing Down the Moon: Witches, Druids, Goddess-worshippers, and other Pagans in America Today.* Boston, MA: Beacon Press.

Akers, Brian Dana, transl. 2002. *The Hatha Yoga Pradipika.* Woodstock, NY: YogaVidya.com. Accessed April 27, 2012 at YogaVidya.com: http://yogavidya.com/Yoga/HathaYogaPradipika.pdf.

Alexiou, Margret. 1974. *The Ritual Lament in Greek Tradition.* London: Cambridge University Press.

Allen, Douglas. 1998. *Myth and Religion in Mircea Eliade.* New York: Garland.

Alley, Kelly. 2002. *On the Banks of Ganga: When Wastewater Meets a Sacred River.* Ann Arbor, MI: University of Michigan Press.

Aquinas, Thomas. 1947. *Summa Theologica.* 3 vols. Translated by the Fathers of the English Dominican Province. New York: Benziger Brothers.

Archer, Margaret S. 2000. *Being Human: The Problem of Agency.* Cambridge: Cambridge University Press.

————. 2007. *Making our Way through the World.* Cambridge: Cambridge University Press.

Archer, Margaret, and Jonathan Tritter. 2000. *Rational Choice Theory: Resisting Colonization.* London: Routledge.

Assmann, Jan. 2006. *Religion and Cultural Memory: Ten Studies.* Stanford, CA: Stanford University Press.

Barker, Chris, and Dariusz Galasiński. 2001. *Cultural Studies and Discourse Analysis.* London: Sage Publications.

Bauman, Zygmunt. 2000. *Liquid Modernity.* Cambridge: Polity.

Beers, Mark H. 2006. "Barriers on the Outside and the Inside." In *The Merck Manual of Medical Information, 2nd Home Edition Online,* edited by

Mark H. Beers. Accessed September 15, 2005 at www.merck.com/ mmhe/index.html.

Bell, Catherine. 1992. *Ritual Theory, Ritual Practice*. New York: Oxford University Press.

———. 1997. *Ritual Perspectives and Dimensions*. New York: Oxford University Press.

———. 2006. "Culture: What Does One Do With It Now?" *Method & Theory in the Study of Religion* 18, no. 4: 315–24.

Benedict XVI. 2007. *Sacramentum Caritatis*, Libreria Editrice Vaticana. Accessed April 27, 2012 at The Holy See: www.vatican.va/ holy_father/benedict_xvi/apost_exhortations/documents/hf_ben-xvi_ exh_20070222_sacramentum-caritatis_en.html.

Bentor, Yael. 2000. "Interiorized Fire Rituals in India and in Tibet." *Journal of the American Oriental Society* 120, no. 4: 594–613.

Berger, Peter, and Stanley Pullberg. 1965. "Reification and the Sociological Critique of Consciousness." *History and Theory* 4, no. 2: 196–211.

Berger, Peter, and Thomas Luckmann. 1967 [1966]. *The Social Construction of Reality*. New York: Anchor Books.

The Holy Bible, New Revised Standard Version, Catholic Edition, Anglicized Text. 2005. London: Darton, Longman and Todd.

Bisschops, Ralph. 1999. "Metaphor as the Internalisation of Ritual – With a Case Study on Samuel Holdheim (1806–1860)." In *Metaphor, Canon and Community: Jewish, Christian and Islamic Approaches*, edited by Ralph Bisschops and James Francis, 284–307. Berne: Peter Lang.

Bodewitz, H. W. 1973. "Agnihotra and Prāṇāgnihotra." In *Jaiminīya Brāhmaṇa I*, 1–65, translated by H. W. Bodewitz. Leiden: Brill.

Bogdan, Henrik. 2007. *Western Esotericism and Rituals of Initiation*. New York: State University of New York Press.

Bowie, Andrew. 2003. *Aesthetics and Subjectivity: From Kant to Nietzsche*. Manchester: Manchester University Press.

Boyer, Pascal. 1994. *The Naturalness of Religious Ideas: A Cognitive Theory of Religion*. Berkeley: University of California Press.

Brient, Elizabeth. 2002. *The Immanence of the Infinite: Hans Blumenberg and the Threshold to Modernity.* Washington D.C.: The Catholic University of America Press.

Brook, Vincent, ed. 2006. *You Should See Yourself: Jewish Identity in Postmodern American Culture.* New Brunswick, NJ: Rutgers University Press.

Brown, Daniel. 2002. "Martyrdom in Sunni Revivalist Thought." In *Sacrificing the Self: Martyrdom in World Religions,* edited by Margaret Cormack. Oxford: Oxford University Press.

Bruck, Gabriele vom, and Barbara Bodenhorn, eds. 2006. *The Anthropology of Names and Naming.* Cambridge: Cambridge University Press.

Brush, Pippa. 1998. "Metaphors of Inscription: Discipline, Plasticity and the Rhetoric of Choice." *Feminist Review* 58: 22–43.

Campbell, Ernest Q. 1964. "The Internalization of Moral Norms." *Sociometry* 27, no. 4: 391–412.

Camus, Albert. 1942. *Le Mythe de Sisyphe.* Paris: Gallimard.

Carlton, Dennis W., and Daniel R. Fischel. 1983. "The Regulation of Insider Trading." *Stanford Law Review* 35, no. 5: 857–95.

Catechism of the Catholic Church. 1994. London: Chapman.

Cavallin, Clemens. 2002. *The Efficacy of Sacrifice: Correspondences in the Ṛgvedic Brahmanas.* Papers Published at the Department of Religious Studies, Gothenburg University, no. 29. Gothenburg: The Department of Religious Studies, Gothenburg University.

————. 2003. "Sacrifice as Action and Actions as Sacrifices: The Role of Breath in the Internalisation of Sacrificial Action in the Vedic Brāhmaṇas." In *Ritualistics,* edited by Tore Ahlbäck. Åbo: Donner Institute for Research in Religious and Cultural History.

Cavallin, Samuel. 1999. *Skuld.* Uppsala: Iustus förlag.

Clarke, Howard. 2003. *Gospel of Matthew and Its Readers: A Historical Introduction to the First Gospel.* Bloomington, IN: Indiana University Press.

Clarke, Scott. 1994. *Japan: A View from the Bath.* Honolulu: University of Hawaii Press.

Dawson, John David. 2001. *Christian Figural Reading and the Fashioning of Identity.* Berkeley: University of California Press.

Delany, J. 1910. "Intention." In *The Catholic Encyclopedia.* New York: Robert

Appleton Company. Accessed April 27, 2012 from New Advent: http://
www.newadvent.org/cathen/08069b.htm.

Delanty, Gerard. 2000. *Modernity and Postmodernity*. London: Sage Publications.

Delumeau, Jean. 1995. *History of Paradise: The Garden of Eden in Myth and Tradition*. New York: Continuum.

Dorward, Frances R. 1985. "The Function of Interiorization in *Oficio de tiniebas*." *Neophilologus* 69, no. 3: 374–85.

Douglas, Mary. 1966. *Purity and Danger: An Analysis of Concepts of Pollution and Taboo*. London: Routledge & Kegan Paul.

———. 1996 [1970]. *Natural Symbols: Explorations in Cosmology*. London: Routledge.

Duff, R. A. 1990. *Intention, Agency and Criminal Liability*. Oxford: Basil Blackwell.

Dundes, Alan. 2002. *The Shabbat Elevator and other Sabbath Subterfuges: An Unorthodox Essay on Circumventing Custom and Jewish Character*. Lanham: Rowman & Littlefield Publishers.

Dunn, Francis M. 1996. *Tragedy's End: Closure and Innovation in Euripidean Drama*. New York: Oxford University Press.

Dupré, Louis. 1993. *Passage to Modernity: An Essay in the Hermeneutics of Nature and Culture*. New Haven and London: Yale University Press.

Eggeling, Julius, transl. 1966 [1882]. *The Shatapatha-Brahmana: According to the Text of Madhyandina School, Part I, Books I and II*. Delhi: Motilal Banarsidass.

Elder-Vass, Dave. 2007. "Luhmann and Emergentism: Competing Paradigms for Social Systems Theory?" *Philosophy of the Social Sciences* 37: 408–32.

Eliade, Mircea. 1970. "Review of 'Alchemy and Science in China' by Nathan Sivin." *History of Religions* 10, no. 2: 178–82.

———. 1973 [1958]. *Yoga: Immortality and Freedom*. Princeton, NJ: Princeton University Press.

Eliade, Mircea, and Lawrence Sullivan. 1987. "Hierophany." In *The Encyclopedia of Religion*. Vol. 6, edited by Mircea Eliade, 313–17. New York: Macmillan Publishing Company.

Encyclopedia of Religion. 1987. Edited by Mircea Eliade. New York: Macmillan Publishing Company.

Etkes, I. 2002. *Gaon of Vilna: The Man and his Image.* Berkeley: University of California Press.

Evans-Pritchard, Edward E. 1937. *Witchcraft, Oracles and Magic among the Azande.* Oxford: Oxford University Press.

Ferguson, Harvie. 2000. *Modernity and Subjectivity: Body, Soul, Spirit.* Charlottesville, VA: University Press of Virginia.

Flood, Gavin. 2002. "The Purification of the Body in Tantric Ritual Representation." *Indo-Iranian Journal* 45: 25–43.

———. 2004. *The Ascetic Self: Subjectivity, Memory and Tradition.* Cambridge: Cambridge University Press.

———. 2006. *The Tantric Body: The Secret Tradition of Hindu Religion.* London: I. B. Taurus.

Gade, Anna. 2002. "Taste, Talent, and the Problem of Internalization: A Qur'ānic study in Religious Musicality from Southeast Asia." *History of Religions* 41, no. 4: 328–66.

Gansten, Martin. 2003. *Patterns of Destiny: Hindu Nādī Astrology.* Lund Studies in History of Religions. Vol. 17, edited by Tord Olsson. Stockholm: Almqvist & Wiksell.

Gelpi, Donald L. 2001. *Firstborn of Many: A Christology for Converting Christians.* Milwaukee, WI: Marquette University Press.

Gillett, Grant R. 2001. *Consciousness and Intentionality.* Philadelphia, PA: John Benjamins Publishing Company.

Gillespie, Michael Allen. 2008. *The Theological Origins of Modernity.* Chicago: University of Chicago Press.

Glynn, Paul. 2003 [1999]. *Healing Fire of Christ: Reflections on Modern Miracles, Lourdes, Knock, Fatima.* San Francisco: Ignatius.

Glucklich, Ariel. 2001. *Sacred Pain: Hurting the Body for the Sake of the Soul.* Oxford: Oxford University Press.

Goldhill, Simon. 2005. *The Temple of Jerusalem,* Cambridge, MA: Harvard University Press.

Grapard, Allen. 1991. "Rule-governed Activity vs. Rule-creating Activity." *Religion* 21: 207–12.

Grimes, Ronald. 1975. "Masking: Toward a Phenomenology of Exteriorization." *Journal of the American Academy of Religion* 43, no. 3: 508–16.

———. 1995 [1982]. *Beginnings in Ritual Studies: Revised Edition.* Columbia, SC: University of South Carolina Press.

———. 2006. *Rite out of Place: Ritual, Media and the Arts.* Oxford: Oxford University Press.

Handelman, Don. 2006. "Framing." In *Theorizing Rituals: Issues, Topics, Approaches, Concepts,* edited by Jens Kreinath, Jan Snoek, and Michael Stausberg. Leiden: Brill.

Hanegraaff, Wouter J. 1998. *New Age Religion and Western Culture: Esotericism in the Mirror of Secular Thought.* Albany, NY: State University of New York Press.

Harrington, Melissa. 2006. "Magical Ritual in Modern Pagan Witchcraft." In *Materializing Religion: Expression, Performance and Ritual,* edited by Elisabeth Arweck and William Keenan. Aldershot, Hampshire: Ashgate.

Hervieu-Léger, Danièle. 2000 [1993]. *Religion as a Chain of Memory.* Oxford: Blackwell.

Holm, Nils G. 1987. "Sundén's Role Theory and Glossolalia." *Journal for the Scientific Study of Religion* 26, no. 3: 383–89.

Humphrey, Caroline, and James Laidlaw. 1994. *The Archetypal Actions of Ritual: A Theory of Ritual Illustrated by the Jain Rite of Worship.* Oxford: Clarendon Press.

———. 2006. "Action." In *Theorizing Rituals: Issues, Topics, Approaches, Concepts,* edited by Jens Kreinath, Jan Snoek, and Michael Stausberg. Leiden: Brill.

Jacobsen, Douglas G. 2003. *Thinking in the Spirit: Theologies of the Early Pentecostal Movement.* Bloomington, IN: Indiana University Press.

Jay, Martin. 1996. "Modernism and the Specter of Psychologism." *Modernism/Modernity,* 3, no. 2: 93–111.

Johnson, Galen A. 1999. "Inside and Outside: Ontological Considerations." In *Merleau-Ponty, Interiority and Exteriority, Psychic Life and the World,* edited by Dorothea Olkowski and James Morley. New York: State University of New York Press.

Jonas, Hans. 1969. "Myth and Mysticism: A Study of Objectification and Interiorization in Religious Thought." *The Journal of Religion* 49: 315–29.

Keller, Catherine. 2002. *Face of the Deep: A Theology of Becoming*. London: Routledge.

Kjellström, Rolf, and Håkan Rydving. 1988. *Den Samiska trumman*. Stockholm: Nordiska museet.

Klawans, Jonathan. 2000. *Impurity and Sin in Ancient Judaism*. Oxford: Oxford University Press.

————. 2002. "Interpreting the Last Supper: Sacrifice, Spiritualization, and Anti-sacrifice." *New Testament Studies* 48: 1–17.

Knott, Kim. 2005. *The Location of Religion: A Spatial Analysis*. London: Equinox.

Kraft, Siv Ellen. 2005. *Den ville kroppen: Tatovering, piercing og smerteritualer i dag*. Oslo: Pax Forlag.

Kreinath, Jens, Constance Hartung and Annette Deschner, eds. 2004. *The Dynamics of Changing Rituals: The Transformation of Religious Rituals within their Social and Cultural Context*. New York: Peter Lang.

Kreinath, Jens. 2005. "Ritual: Theoretical Issues in the Study of Religion." *Revista de Estudos da Religião* 5, no. 4. Accessed May 13, 2008, www.pucsp.br/rever/rv4_2005/t_kreinath.htm.

Kugle, Scott A. 2003. "The Heart of Ritual Is the Body: Anatomy of an Islamic Devotional Manual of the Nineteenth Century." *Journal of Ritual Studies* 17, no. 1: 42–60.

Lakoff, George, and Mark Johnson. 2003 [1980]. *Metaphors We Live By*. Chicago: University of Chicago Press.

Launderville, Dale. 2004. "Ezekiel's Throne-Chariot Vision: Spiritualizing the Model of Divine Royal Rule (On an Understanding of Transcendent Cosmic Order through the Interiorization of Political Power)." *The Catholic Biblical Quarterly* 66, no. 3: 361–77.

Lavine, T. Z. 1981. "Internalization, Socialization, and Dialectic." *Philosophy and Phenomenological Research* 42, no. 1: 91–110.

Leder, Drew. 1990. *The Absent Body*. Chicago: University of Chicago Press.

Levy, Neil. 2002. *Moral Relativism: A Short Introduction*. Oxford: Oneworld.

Løgstrup, Knud. 1995. *Metaphysics*. Vol. 2, translated by Russell L. Dees. Milwaukee, WI: Marquette University Press.

Löwendahl, Lena. 2002. *Med kroppen som instrument: En studie av new age med fokus på hälsa, kroppslighet och genus*. Lund Studies in History of Religions. Vol. 15, edited by Tord Olsson. Lund: Religionshistoriska avdelningen, Lund University.

Luhmann, Niklas. 1982 [1971–77]. *The Differentiation of Society*, translated by Stephen Holmes and Charles Larmore. New York: Columbia University Press.

———. 1995 [1984]. *Social Systems*, translated by John Bednarz. Stanford, CA: Stanford University Press.

Mack, Burton L. 1991. "Staal's Gauntlet and the Queen." *Religion* 21: 213–18.

Makin, Gideon. 2000. *Metaphysicians of Meaning: Russell and Frege on Sense and Denotation*. London: Routledge.

Martin, Emily. 1992. "The End of the Body?" *American Ethnologist* 19, no. 1: 121–40.

Matheus, Robert. 2006. "On Ministerial Intention." Accessed February 15, 2006 from Ecclesia Dei: www.ecclesiadei.nl/apologetiek/ministeralintentions.html.

Mcguire, Meredith B. 1990. "Religion and the Body: Rematerializing the Human Body in the Social Sciences of Religion." *Journal for the Scientific Study of Religion* 29, no. 3: 283–96.

McKeon, Michael, ed. 2000. *Theory of the Novel: A Historical Approach*. Baltimore, MD: The Johns Hopkins University Press.

Michaels, Axel. 2006. "Ritual and Meaning." In *Theorizing Rituals: Issues, Topics, Approaches, Concepts*, edited by Jens Kreinath, Jan Snoek and Michael Stausberg. Leiden: Brill.

Millet, L. 1978. "Remarques sur l'intériorité et l'intériorisation." *Annales medico-psychologiques* 136, no. 5: 796–802.

Mir-Hosseini, Ziba. 2006. *Islam and Democracy in Iran: Eshkevari and the Quest for Reform*. London: I. B. Tauris & Company.

Morinis, Alan. 1985. "The Ritual Experience: Pain and the Transformation of Consciousness in Ordeals of Initiation." *Ethos* 13, no. 2: 150–74.

Ogden, Daniel. 2002. *Magic, Witchcraft, and Ghosts in the Greek and Roman Worlds: A Sourcebook*. Oxford: Oxford University Press.

Olivelle, Patrick, trans. 1998. *The Early Upanisads: Annotated Text and Translation*. New York: Oxford University Press.

Oort, Richard. 2006. "Shakespeare and the Idea of the Modern." *New Literary History* 37, no. 2: 319–39.

Origen. 1989. *Commentary on the Gospel According to John, Books 1–10*. Translated by Ronald E. Heine. The Fathers of the Church, edited by Thomas P. Halton, vol. 80. Washington: The Catholic University of America Press.

Orsi, Robert A. 2005. *Between Heaven and Earth*. Princeton, NJ: Princeton University Press.

Osho. 2005. "The OSHO Mystic Rose Meditation: Laughter, Tears, and Silence." Accessed November 22, 2005 from Osho: www.osho.com/Topics/TopicsEng/MysticRose.htm.

Oxford English Dictionary. 2005. Oxford: Oxford University Press. Accessed March 14, 2007 from: http://dictionary.oed.com.

Palmer, Norris. 2005. "Baba's World: A Global Guru and his Movement." In *Gurus in America*, edited by Thomas A. Forsthoefel and Cynthia Ann Humes. New York: State University of New York Press.

Pardee, Dennis. 2003. "Ugaritic Extispicy." In *Context of Scripture: Canonical Compositions, Monumental Inscriptions and Archival Documents from the Biblical World*. Vol. 3, edited by William Hallo. Leiden: Koninklijke Boekhandel en Drukkerij.

Patton, Kimberley. 2009. *Religion of the Gods: Ritual, Paradox, and Reflexivity*. Oxford: Oxford University Press.

Pancavimsa Brahmana. 1934–35. Edited by A. Chinaswāmi Shāstri. Kāshi Sanskrit Series, no. 105. Benares: Sanskrit Series Office.

Penner, Hans. 1985. "Language, Ritual and Meaning." *Numen* 32: 1–16.

Pitkin, Hanna Fenichel. 1987. "Rethinking Reification." *Theory and Society* 16, no. 2: 263–93.

Preston, James J. 1987. "Purification." In *The Encyclopedia of Religion*. Vol. 12, edited by Mircea Eliade, 91–100. New York: Macmillan Publishing Company.

Pyysiäinen, Ilkka. 2003. *How Religion Works: Towards a New Cognitive Science of Religion*. Brill: Leiden.

Rappaport, Roy. 1997. *Ritual and Religion in the Making of Humanity*. Cambridge: Cambridge University Press.

Ricoeur, Paul. 1973. "The Model of the Text: Meaningful Action Considered as a Text." *New Literary History* 5, no. 1: 91–117.

Rickman, H. P. 1988. *Dilthey Today: A Critical Appraisal of the Contemporary Relevance of his Work*. New York: Greenwood Press.

Rippin, Andrew. 1993. *Muslims: Their Religious Beliefs and Practices: The Contemporary Period*. Vol. 2. London: Routledge.

Rozik, Eli. 2002. *The Roots of Theatre: Rethinking Ritual and other Theories of Origin*. Iowa City, IA: University of Iowa Press.

Saso, Michael. 1997. "The Taoist Body and Cosmic Prayer." In *Religion and the Body*, edited by Sarah Coakley, 231–47. Cambridge: Cambridge University Press.

Sawyer, John F. 1999. *Sacred Languages and Sacred Texts*. London: Routledge.

Schafer, Roy. 1968. *Aspects of Internalization*. New York: International Universities Press.

Schechner, Richard. 1987. "A Vedic Ritual in Quotation Marks." *The Journal of Asian Studies* 46, no. 1: 108–10.

Schilling, Chris. 2004. *Body in Culture, Technology and Society*. London: Sage Publications.

Scott, John Finley. 1971. *Internalization of Norms: A Sociological Theory of Moral Commitment*. Englewood Cliffs: Prentice-Hall.

Segal, Robert A. 2006. "Myth and Ritual." In *Theorizing Rituals: Issues, Topics, Approaches, Concepts*, edited by Jens Kreinath, Jan Snoek, and Michael Stausberg. Leiden: Brill.

Seligman, Adam, Robert Weller, Michael Puett, and Simon Bennett. 2008. *Ritual and its Consequences: An Essay on the Limits of Sincerity*. Oxford: Oxford University Press.

Singer, Philip. 1990. "'Psychic Surgery': Close Observation of a Popular Healing Practice." *Medical Anthropology Quarterly*, n.s., 4, no. 4: 443–51.

Smith, Brian K. 1991. "Review of Rules Without Meaning by Frits Staal." *Journal of Ritual Studies* 5, no. 2: 141–43.

————. 1998 [1989]. *Reflections on Resemblance, Ritual, and Religion.* Delhi: Motilal Banarsidass.

Sørensen, Jesper. 2006. *A Cognitive Theory of Magic.* Lanham, MD: Altamira.

Spero, Moshe Halevi. 1999. "A Brief Note on Ingram's (1997) Concept of Interiorization." *The American Journal of Psychoanalysis* 59, no. 2: 171–74.

Sperry, Paul. 2005. *Infiltration: How Muslim Spies and Subversives Have Penetrated Washington.* Washington: Nelson Current.

Staal, Frits. 1961. *Advaita and Neoplatonism.* Madras: Madras University.

————. 1989. *Rules Without Meaning: Ritual, Mantras and the Human Sciences.* New York: Peter Lang.

————. 1993. "From Meanings to Trees." *Journal of Ritual Studies* 7, no. 2: 11–32.

Staal, Frits, C. V. Somayajipadandand, and M. Itti Ravi. Nambudiri. 1983. *Agni: The Vedic Ritual of the Fire Altar.* 2 vols. Berkeley, CA: Asian Humanities Press.

Stark, Rodney, and William Sims Bainbridge. 1996 [1987]. *A Theory of Religion.* New Brunswick, NJ: Rutgers University Press.

Stausberg, Michael. 2002. "Ritteorier och religionsteorier." In *Riter och Ritteorier: Religionshistoriska diskussioner och teoretiska ansatser,* edited by Michael Stausberg, Olof Sundqvist, and Lydia Svalastog. Nora: Nya Doxa.

————. 2006. "Reflexivity." In *Theorizing Rituals: Issues, Topics, Approaches, Concepts,* edited by Jens Kreinath, Jan Snoek, and Michael Stausberg. Leiden: Brill.

Strenski, Ivan. 1991. "What's Rite?" *Religion* 21: 219–25.

Stroll, Avrum. 1998. "Proper Names, Names, and Fictive Objects." *The Journal of Philosophy* 95, no. 10: 522–34.

Stryker, S. 2001. "Social Psychology, Sociological." In *International Encyclopedia of the Social & Behavioral Sciences* edited by Neil J. Smelser and Paul B. Baltes. Amsterdam: Elsevier: 14409–14413.

Taylor, Charles. 1991. *The Ethics of Authenticity.* Cambridge, MA: Harvard University Press.

————. 2002. *Varieties of Religion Today: William James Revisited*. Cambridge, MA: Harvard University Press.

Tucker, Karen B. Westerfield 2001. *American Methodist Worship*. Oxford: Oxford University Press.

Turner, Victor. 1988. *The Anthropology of Performance*. New York: PAJ publications.

————. 1994 [1967]. *The Forest of Symbols: Aspects of Ndembu Ritual*. Ithaca, NY: Cornell University Press.

Tweed, Thomas A. 2006. *Crossing and Dwelling: A Theory of Religion*. Cambridge, MA: Harvard University Press.

Vanderveken, Daniel, and Susumo Kubo, eds. 2001. *Essays in Speech Act Theory*. Amsterdam/Philadelphia, PA: John Benjamins Publishing.

Wallace, Jennifer. 2007. *The Cambridge Introduction to Tragedy*. Cambridge: Cambridge University Press.

Wallerstein, Immanuel. 1995. "The End of What Modernity?" *Theory and Society* 24, no. 4: 471–88.

Wallis, Kenneth, and James Poulton. 2001. *Internalization: The Origins and Construction of Internal Reality*. Philadelphia, PA: Buckingham Open University Press.

Watson, James. 2007. "Orthopraxy Revisited." *Modern China* 33, no. 1: 154–58.

Weber, Max. 2001 [1920, 1930]. *Protestant Ethic and the Spirit of Capitalism*, translated by Talcott Parsons. London: Routledge.

————. 2003 [1921–22]. "The Types of Legitimate Domination." In *Theories of Social Order: A Reader*, edited by Michael Hechter. Palo Alto, CA: Stanford University Press.

Werner, Eric. 2000. "Ontogeny of the Social Self: Towards a Formal Computational Theory." In *Human Cognition and Social Agent Technology*, edited by Kerstin Dautenhahn, 263–300. Philadelphia, PA: John Benjamins Publishing Company.

Whitmore Charles E. 1919. "The Nature of Tragedy." *Publications of the Modern Language Association of America* 34, no. 3: 341–59.

Woods, Tim. 1999. *Beginning Postmodernism*. Manchester: Manchester University Press.

Yates, Nigel. 1999. *Anglican Ritualism in Victorian Britain 1830–1910*. Oxford: Oxford University Press.

Zink, Sidney. 1963. "The Meaning of Proper Names." *Mind*, n.s., 72, no. 288: 481–99.

Index

www.ingramcontent.com/pod-product-compliance
Lightning Source LLC
Chambersburg PA
CBHW031128020426
42333CB00012B/273